THE POSSIBILITIES
OF THE
NEGRO IN SYMPOSIUM

THE POSSIBILITIES
OF THE
NEGRO IN SYMPOSIUM

By

Charles E. Dowman,

John Temple Graves, and others

The Black Heritage Library Collection

BOOKS FOR LIBRARIES PRESS
FREEPORT, NEW YORK
1971

First Published 1904
Reprinted 1971

Reprinted from a copy in the
Fisk University Library Negro Collection

INTERNATIONAL STANDARD BOOK NUMBER:
0-8369-8902-3

LIBRARY OF CONGRESS CATALOG CARD NUMBER:
75-173610

PRINTED IN THE UNITED STATES OF AMERICA
BY
NEW WORLD BOOK MANUFACTURING CO., INC.
HALLANDALE, FLORIDA 33009

The Possibilities of the Negro in Symposium

REV. C. E. DOWMAN, D.D.,
HON. JOHN TEMPLE GRAVES,
HENRY W. GRADY,
EX-GOVERNOR W. J. NORTHEN,
BISHOP WARREN A. CANDLER, D.D., LL.D.,
BISHOP H. M. TURNER, D.D., LL.D.,
BISHOP L. H. HOLSEY, D.D.,
RICHARD H. EDMONDS,
WILLIS B. PARKS, M.D.

A Solution of the Negro Problem Psychologically Considered. The Negro Not "A Beast."

The Franklin Printing and Publishing Company
ATLANTA, GA.

CONTENTS.

FOREWORD.

By CHAS. E. DOWMAN, D.D.,
Ex-President Emory College, Oxford.

The negro is with us, much has been said and written, but the last word has not yet been spoken, for "nothing is settled, till it is settled right." After the strife of words and the ebullition of passion, right and truth will remain. No doubt, much that was unwise and untrue has been said. Men have discussed this question from the viewpoint of prejudice, passion, and personal interest as well as from sincere, though often misdirected philanthropy. But many of the highest minds have carefully considered this problem; some are still seeking for a solution; others have thought it through, and from their premises have reached a conclusion.

Dr. Willis B. Parks, the author of the essay which closes this volume, has rendered a service to the thinking public by collecting and putting in permanent form the mature thought of some of the leading men of both races, as well as by his own contribution to the discussion of this question. The study of the negro from a psychological standpoint, gives promise of a better understanding of the peculiarities of his character and conduct that have been difficult to explain, and furnishes valuable suggestions of more intelligent methods for his improvement. The author, with scientific candor and firmness, seeks to check any tendency toward dehumanizing the negro by showing from the application of the principles of psychology that he is "not a beast," but a man.

The eloquent and big-hearted Henry W. Grady, and the concise and brilliant John Temple Graves, need no introduction or commendation. The pure and patriotic William J. Northen enjoys the confidence of all races and sections.

The masterful bishop of the Methodist Episcopal Church, South, Warren A. Candler, pleads for justice toward the negro as opposed to the mob. The earnest and observant bishop of the African Methodist Church, Henry M. Turner, agrees that this question can only be settled by the separation of the races, and Rev. L. H. Holsey, D.D., the eloquent and big-hearted bishop of the Colored M. E. Church, pleads for the segregation of the race in some portion of our national domain.

Richard H. Edmonds, editor of the "Manufacturers' Record," an astute man of business, holds that if wily politicians and sentimental philanthropists will let this problem alone, the two races will probably work out its solution.

Many say they are tired of this discussion—but certain things are true: The negro is here, and here to stay, and so long as there is the want of perfect adjustment between him and the white race, there will be the *problem*, and so long as there is a problem, there will be a discussion.

The position of the negro race is more critical now than at any former period of its history. During the time immediately succeeding emancipation, there was a kindly and sympathetic relation between the white people of the South and their former slaves. But with the passing of the old masters and the old servants, with the coming of generations who know nothing of the sentiments of affection and gratitude growing out of the relations of domestic slavery, and who have been reared under the influence of passion on the one side and suspicion on the other, it was inevitable that the races should drift apart.

The Southern white man has easily lost confidence in the negro. The increase of crime, the comparative failure of education, the frequent divorcement of religion from morality, the menace to the safety of the home and of innocent women from the rapist have turned the feelings of many white men from sympathetic helpfulness to strained toleration.

It would be putting the case very mildly to say that the negro's most enthusiastic friends in the North are disappointed in him. His moral and social progress has not been what they expected as a result of their investment of money and help. The laboring classes of the North will not admit him. The doors of social life are closed against him. Since the Southern States have, as a matter of self-preservation, practically eliminated him from politics, whose affection for "the man and brother" was prompted by self-interest, has no further use for him.

With the North indifferent and the South unsympathetic, the negro would be crushed between the upper and the nether millstone. But his future is in his own hands. Content with his civil liberty, enjoying educational advantages at the cost of his white neighbors, with a fair field for his industry, not excluded from the ranks of skilled labor, with the fields, the forests, the mines of the South, begging for him with the monopoly of domestic service, he is in position to make rapid progress in the accumulation of property, the building of homes, and in the elevation of his social condition.

The South will not have him as a social equal nor as a political master, but she needs him, and wants him as a powerful factor in her industrial prosperity. His labor augments her wealth, his growing demand for the necessity of civilized life makes a market for her products, his increase of population gives proportionate influence in national legislation.

Bishop Galloway, one of the most eloquent preachers of the Methodist church, said in a public address a few months ago, that when the negro left the South he would go with him, and the utterance was received with enthusiastic applause.

The South is willing to give the negro a chance. As the ward of the nation he has been spoiled; as the football of demagogues he has been corrupted. As the pet of sentimental philanthropists he has been placed in a false and dangerous position. As the prey of the avaricious, his vices have been fostered for their gain.

What the future has for him depends on himself. The sky is clearing. The views of all sections and parties are coming nearer together. The wisest men of the negro race are recognizing the time basis of his salvation. His best friends, who are among the white people of the South, are ready to help him under practical ways.

What shall we do with him shall no longer be discussed. With equality before the law, with equity in business, with sympathy in all his efforts to better his condition on all proper lines, instead of being a menace to our safety, a disturbing element in our politics, and a peril to himself, he may become a race unit in our great cosmopolitan national life, "separate as the billows, but not as the sea," and under the benign influence of the gospel of the Son of man, our civilization may show the possibility of which has been declared impossible—a superior and an inferior race living and working together in true harmony and cooperation.

THE PROBLEM OF THE RACES.

By JOHN TEMPLE GRAVES.

(Chicago University Speech.)

Mr. President, Ladies and Gentlemen:

Permit me in the beginning to acknowledge the courtesy which gives me access to a platform so noble and to an audience so distinguished as this.

All sections of our common country pay tribute to the merit and equipment of this splendid University. Its work is playing a mighty part in the educational uplift of the times. Its record has been notable among the forces which have given us a reunited country. The State and the section from which I come have made their yearly vital contribution to its student-roll, and the superb beneficence of the founder, joined to the noble liberality of citizens of Chicago, and to the consecrated talent and attainments of its faculty, have made an institution so virile in life, so comprehensive in character, and so national in scope that it has come, while yet in early youth, to be the *alma mater* of the sections and the pride of the republic.

Fortunate am I, and happy, in that I bring the convictions of this hour to a platform so free, and to an atmosphere so impartial. Questions of abstract policy—problems of humanity—bearing a hint of section or a complication of party are not for the ears of faction or for the passions of politics. Upon the fierce and heated bosom of established prejudice the cold stream of reason falls too frequently to steam and hissing, and men who have convictions that are rather definite than popular, may thank God for the calmer air of universities, and for the clear and unbiased minds of students seeking truth. It is here, and here only, that problems of duty and of destiny can find a fair hearing and a free solution in the tranquil temper and unfettered vision of republican youth.

Upon this dear presumption I hasten to my work.

The problem which I bring to you to-day is yours as well as mine. Whoever you are, and from whatever section you come, the problem is yours—inherited from the fathers and handed down to the sons—with complications increasing so rapidly, and difficulties multiplying so fast that every instinct of prudence, and every suggestion of safety plead for its prompt and full consideration, while it may yet be solved—a problem for the whole country, because it can not be settled by a section; and a problem for this generation, because in this generation it must inevitably reach its crisis and advance in promise or decline in evil presage to its conclusion.

The thinkers of the Old World, from Gladstone and Bismarck, through James Bryce and Arthur Balfour, to Chamberlain and Crispi, viewing our country from the vantage ground of distance, have with one voice proclaimed this the first and foremost problem of our national life.

The thinkers of our own world, who see the problem clearly, are appalled at the comprehensive danger of its elements, and amazed at the apathy of their countrymen toward it.

Will you bear with me, then, while I state this problem briefly and as fairly as I can?

The Civil War of the sixties was the tragedy of the nineteenth century. Its real cause dated back to constitutional constructions, and to the irrepressible conflict over the nature of the compact framed by the fathers. Its provoking incident, its precipitating cause, was slavery.

A republic of white men, living in a country developed and established by sturdy colonists of the Anglo-Saxon race, prospering under a constitution framed by white men—for the author of the Declaration was a slaveholder—flourishing magnificently under institutions molded by their united brains, cemented by their common blood, and sanctified by their common patriotism—fell at outs over a black man brought from savage Africa and sold from trading ships to bondage and slavery, first in Massachusetts, and afterwards in the South. We do not halt here to wrangle over the mooted responsibility of his bringing, or the causes of his subsequent concentration in one section of the country. He came, he drifted, and he divided us. Agitators, sincere but passionate, raised the question of his liberty. The sections divided in interest and sentiment upon the issue, and over his black body brethren of a white race and of a common glorious heritage went to war.

Of equal valor, but of unequal numbers, the men of the North and the men of the South grappled for four years at each other's throats; and for this black man of Africa the white men of America sacrificed a million heroic lives and spent $12,000,000,000 of their money.

Whether it were worth the colossal sacrifice, history, and one hundred thousand broken homes, must in time declare. And whether the sacrifice were vain and profitless, history and the unsolved problem must also say.

From the unequal contest one section emerged victorious, and the other section lingered solemn and broken in defeat.

The first act of the victor was to free the slaves. The next act of the victor was to make the black man, just now a slave, a citizen and the equal of his master. There were four million black men then. There are nine million now, and seven million in the South.

Here, then, the equations start:

Two opposite, unequal, and antagonistic races are set side by side for government and destiny. One of these, by the record, is the strongest race on earth; the other, by the record, is the weakest race on earth. One, a race whose achievements make, in large part, the history of the world; the other, a race which, in all its annals, has written no history, built no monuments, made no books, and recorded no achievement, and whose only progress has been from contact with the stronger race. One, a race, proud, progressive, dominant, and historically free; the other, a race that came out of centuries of savagery into centuries of slavery, and was transplanted in one tropical and unnatural night from barbarism and slavery into liberty and full equality. One, a live, vital, twentieth-century race, pulsing the hope and progress of the world; the other, a race without a record, undeveloped, untrained, but lately slaves, and at the utmost a seventh-century civilization.

There they are—master and slave, civilized and half-civilized, strong and weak, conquering and servile, twentieth-century and seventh-century— thirteen hundred years apart—set by a strange and incomprehensible edict of statesmanship or of passion, set by the constitution and the law, the weakest race on earth and the strongest race on earth, side by side, on equal terms to bear an equal part in the conduct and responsibility of the greatest government the world ever saw!

It was an experiment without a precedent in history and without a promise in the annals of man.

Impracticable in abstract form, the proposition is rendered impossible by its complications. The master race keenly resents the sudden elevation and the forced equality of their slaves. The victorious section eagerly demands the trial, and desires the success of its experiment. The master race, from long contact and close association, carries the ineradicable conviction of the inherent and incurable inferiority and incapacity of the black man. The victor section, reasoning from abstract philanthropy at the distance of a thousand miles, cherishes a fixed faith in the unity of race and the equality of man. Sectional jealousies compass the experiment with bitterness. Partisan politics complicate it with selfish schemes. Frequent crimes and recurring violence distort it with passion. And behind it all, openly confessed in one section, and only half denied in the other section, there lives and breathes in both races and in all sections, the deep, uncircumscribed, and apparently ineradicable *prejudice* of opposite races, which renders union and sympathy and full co-operation hopeless and out of the question forever.

So that the problem is one of irreconcilable elements. It is one of impossible conditions. Stated in a sentence, this is the problem: How the strongest of races and the weakest of races, thirteen hundred years apart in civilization, unequal in history and development, incongruous, unassimilable and inherently antagonistic, tossed between party schemes and sectional jealousies, irritated by racial conflicts and misled by mistaken philanthropy, can live on equal terms under exactly the same laws, and share on equal terms in the same government—when no other races, opposite and antagonistic, have ever shared, in peace and tranquility, since the world began, any country or any government created by God or fashioned by man.

This is the question that the times are called to answer. This is the riddle that the twentieth century is asked to read. This is the experiment that the temporizing statesmanship of a civil revolution has forced upon the age.

The statement of the proposition carries its condemnation, and the equations must be changed before the problem can be solved.

The experiment has had thirty-eight years of trial, backed by the power of the federal government and by the sympathy of the world. It has failed. From the beginning to the hour that holds us, it has failed. The races are wider apart and more antagonistic than they were in 1865. There is less of sympathy and more of tension than the races have known since the terrible days of reconstruction made chaos in the South. The Fifteenth Amendment is practically repealed. In nearly every State of his numerical habitation, the negro is disfranchised under the forms of law. In all the States where his ballot is a menace to white supremacy, it is restrained. With all these years, and all these forces at his back, there has been an utter failure to establish the negro in a satisfactory and self-reliant position under the law. Four decades after his emancipation he is in point of fact less a freeman and infinitely less a citizen than he was in 1868. The tumult of the times about us proclaim the continued existence and the unreconciled equations of the problem that he makes; and in the common judgment of mankind the legend, FAILURE, is written large and lowering above the tottering fabric of his civil rights.

And yet the experiment goes on. Unchanging and unlearning, the republic gropes in solemn stupidity, in helpless apathy, in misguided philanthropy, through ceaseless complications and hopeless precedent to the hopeless and preordained conclusion. The experiment goes on.

I ask you, men and women of this University, to consider with me the difficulties which this vast problem entails, and the mighty reasons which, for the sake of both races, sternly and imperatively require its solution.

To the white man this problem means division. It imperils national unity. It always has done so. It always will do so. From the Philadelphia convention to the present hour the negro has always been a bone of contention. North, East and West, the sections tolerate in tranquility divisions of trade and sentiment, and clasp hands everywhere without suspicion or distrust. But a Chinese wall of prejudice shuts out the South on this question from the sympathy of the American people, and although fraternal platitudes may cross it, and political affiliations may scale it, and commercial interchange may run its electric wires under and above it, and although but recently military loyalty has seemed to shatter it, this wall stands, in the sight of God and of nations, and hedges in the South as a separate and peculiar people, hindered with misapprehension, held aloof in prejudice, and fretted by a criticism which, if sometimes founded in philanthropy, is too often expressed in passion and answered in bitterness.

And so long as the problem stands the old slave States of the South, unwillingly, protestingly, despairingly, and yet inevitably, must be, and will be, the continuing gap in the magnificent line of our national unity.

To the white man of the South the problem hampers its material development. It halts our growth. By the records of the census it frightens immigration from industrial competition with the negro. It largely deters capital from investment in the shadow of an unsolved problem. It makes a standard of labor that prejudices all our Southern poor against menial but honorable service. It depresses agriculture on the farms and property in the suburbs, and drives all who can afford the change to the safety afforded by proximity and police protection in the cities. The South is unequaled in the four great basic raw materials of coal, iron, cotton and lumber. And yet, while $100,000,000 of our money goes yearly to Europe at 4 per cent., these great fields are scantily developed. And thus, while one great section of our country is halted in development, the free movement of men and money in all sections is hindered toward the inviting field of opportunity.

It is a problem of moral decay. It demoralizes politics. Wherever a black supremacy is threatened through a black majority the black ballot is strangled without reserve in the black hands that hold it against the safety of the State. This is wrong. It is illegal. It is monstrous. But it is true. It is true in Georgia. It is true in South Carolina. Aye, and it would be true in Massachusetts and in Illinois. Put yourself, men of Illinois, in the place of the people you perhaps condemn. Suppose that by the steady drift of emigration the negro had come from the South to be a majority in every congressional district, in every legislative precinct, and in every municipal ward of Illinois. Suppose that, realizing this majority, he had organized to utilize it. Suppose that you looked forward, in the next election, not only to the probability, but to the absolute certainty, that the next governor of Illinois would be a negro; that you would have two negroes in the United States Senate to take the places of Hopkins and of Cullom; that you would have a solid negro delegation in Congress; a legislature at Springfield looking like a blackbird pie; negro judges on the bench; negro solicitors in your courts; negro mayors in your chairs, and a negro policeman on your streets—let me ask you, man of Illinois, with your pride in the past glories, and your confidence in the future achievements of your historic State—let me ask you, if, in the shadow of this threat and danger, the streets of Springfield and Chicago, and the woods and prairies of Illinois, would not be filled with eager white men asking how the South suppressed the negro vote?

And will you answer that frank question, man of Illinois, or man of Massachusetts, like an honest Caucasian, and like an Anglo-Saxon gentleman?

But the stern and solemn necessity does not cure the moral stain. The deadliest influence that can compass a popular government is in the decay of the spirit that hedges the ballot with sanctity. The ballot is the palladium of our liberties. The ballot is sacred. A crime against the ballot is a stab at the constitution, and the necessity which makes the ballot the sport of conditions must be removed if the republic shall survive. And yet the problem shows no promise on this line. We might as well be honest here. We might as well face stern facts with fearless frankness. I do not say it is right. I know it is wrong. I do not defend. I do not justify. I do not argue it at all. But I am simply here to tell you plainly, definitely, resolutely, from the fulness and certainty of knowledge, that which you already know, and that which, under reversed conditions, you would unquestionably endorse—that there will never come a change in these suppressions while these conditions last.

Never, never in a thousand years will the negro,

North or South, be allowed to govern in this republic, even where his majorities are plain. We might as well fix this fact in our minds to stay. No statute can eradicate, no public opinion can remove, no armed force can overthrow, the inherent, invincible, indestructible, and, if you will, the unscrupulous capacity and determination of the Anglo-Saxon race to rule.

It is only the knife of surgery that can cure this poison in the body and the bones of politics. Under the shadow of the problem our politics must, and will, be stained.

Good government at this point, and wherever this black ballot is counted, is threatened, too, in its integrity by the growing numbers and the increasing venality of this mercenary and irresponsible and ever-purchasable vote, prolific of corruption, balancing between factions, and holding the mighty power of decision in tremendous issues at the beck of a tribe or the swell of a savage prejudice.

The problem also throttles political independence in the South. We have been ready there for years to divide on party lines. We do not dare to do it. With the white race divided, the negro is held up once more to the ballot-box and becomes the balance of power in the policies of the time. We have our separate and divergent convictions on economic issues. We crush these under the iron heel of necessity. We have our varying interests that would naturally be expressed in opposing politics. We sacrifice these material issues to the greater stake. And the great people of the South, dominated and solidified by the fear of this unwholesome balance, are whipped, protesting, into line behind expediency, and forced to compulsory union in a single party. The education of the hustings, the friction of ideas, the vigilant watchfulness of jealous partisanship, and the political liberty of the thinker and of the voter, are all lost in the shadow of the somber apprehension.

In a land of light and liberty, in an age of enlightenment and law, the women of the South are prisoners to danger and fear. While your women may walk from suburb to suburb, and from township to township, without escort and without alarm, there is not a woman of the South, wife or daughter, who would be permitted, or who would dare to walk at twilight unguarded through the residence streets of a populous town, or to ride the outside highways at midday. The terror of the twilight deepens with the darkness, and in the rural regions every farmer leaves his home with apprehension in the morning and thanks God when he comes from the fields at evening to find all well with the women of his home. For behind the prejudice of race stalks the fiend of lust, and behind the rapist thunders the mob—engine of vengeance, monstrous, lawless, deplorable, but, under the uncured defects of the law the fiery terror of the criminal and the chief defense of woman.

This is also a problem of justice. Fair as our designs, and equitable as our verdicts, as tested by the highest courts, the prejudice of race inevitably poisons law and tempts justice, from the jury's box to the judge's bench.

It is a problem of religious unity—separating brethren and dividing usefulness. For more than one great religious body in this country, cherishing a common creed, believing in one Lord, one faith, one baptism, are sundered and set in separate and sectional camps by the clash of convictions here.

It is a problem of numbers. Four million slaves were freed. There are nine million negroes now. The problem grows in difficulty with marvelously increasing numbers, and is magnified in vitality by delay. If antagonisms, now so fundamental, are not softened; if prejudices, now so serious, are not healed, then the future darkens, and we shall enter with swollen numbers upon a period of strife and wrangle, in whose perils our present troubles will not be remembered. Optimism is easy. Optimism is popular. But the logic of conditions is ominous with warning, and it is braver to be honest and wiser to be prepared.

Here, then, the issues: Unity of the republic, material development, purity of politics, political independence, respect for the ballot, reverence for the constitution, the safety of our homes, the sanctity of our women, the supremacy of law, the sacredness of justice, the integrity of race, and the unity of the church. There is not a phase of our civilization, there is not a principle of our race, there is not a fundamental of society, that is not wrapped in the hopeless tangle which this problem weaves.

These are difficulties which compass the white man of the South. Heaven knows they are serious enough.

But what of the negro? It would be cruel and unkind to cast up the balances of this great account without considering him. I speak the representative sentiment of the South when I say that we would not come to the consideration of this tremendous issue without a high and humane consideration for the negro. How does the problem come to him, and what does the future hold?

"Will the white man permit the negro to have an equal part in the industrial, political, social and civil advantages of the United States?" This, as I understand it, is the question which involves his life and destiny.

These words come from a negro—the wisest, the most thoughtful, and the most eloquent negro of his time—as discreet as Washington, a deeper thinker, and a much more eloquent man. But for one hour of the Atlanta exposition, Council, of Huntsville, might stand to-day where Washington, of Tuskegee stands—as the recognized leader of his race.

This question, asked by Council, as the deliberate representative of his people, is the core of the negro problem.

The answer to it is in every white man's heart, even if it does not lie openly on every white man's lips. It may be expressed in diplomacy; it may be veiled in indirection; it may be softened in philanthropy; it may be guarded in politic utterance, and oftenest of all, it is restrained by ultra conservatism and personal timidity. But wherever the answer to this vital question comes, stripped of verbiage and indirection, it rings like a martial bugle in the single syllable—"No!"

This may not be right, but it is honest. It may not be just, but it is evident. It may not be politic, but it is a great, glaring, indisputable, indestructible fact. North and South, the answer, wherever it is honest, is the same. I agree with Albion Tourgee that there are not ten thousand men in the republic who can answer that question in the affirmative. Council knows the answer and states it with the courage of a man. Bishop Turner knows it; Bishop Holsey knows it; Bryden and Bruce and Taylor knew it; the Chicago papers know it; I think that Booker T. Washington knows it sadly in his heart, and I believe that every thoughtful gentleman who strips theory from the bare form of fact knows it—here and everywhere.

This is from first to last a race problem. It is an issue of race and not of politics. It is a thing of skin and type, and not of section or condition. It is a part of the universal problem. The history of man has been written in a race antagonism and in race separation. The Hebrew and Egyptian, the Jew and the

Gentile, the Turk and the Christian, Magyar and Hungarian, Venetian and Moor, Mexican and Texan, negro and Chinaman, white man and Indian—the repulsion is the same.

A thousand years have not removed the prejudice against the Jew, who is the aristocrat of history. How then shall the negro hope to conquer where the Jew has failed? This race prejudice has no sectional lines. It is held in no geographical boundaries. Every issue of the leading negro papers published in the North reeks with protest against the discriminations exercised throughout the North against the negro race. Boston, the metropolis of abolition, will not employ negroes in the department stores. Nor will Chicago. The Boston "Globe" received a formal social protest against the employment of a negro reporter on its local staff. The sister's son of Wendell Phillips, rich with the evangel blood of emancipation, refused to associate with a negro in Harvard University. Fred Douglas in his last speech declared that only one white man in all the ranks of the abolitionists had ever permitted him to forget in his presence that he was a negro. There are 40,000 negroes in Ohio, Pennsylvania and New York. Where is the office that they hold, or the station of trust and profit that they fill? In Mr. Crumpacker's State of Indiana they lynch negroes almost as frequently and upon much less provocation than in Georgia. A riot raised on race prejudice reddened the central avenues of New York. Chicago citizens chased a negro through the central streets, ready with a rope to visit capital punishment for theft. Boston elected a negro by accident to her common council, and then offered him $10,000 to remove his offensive color from the chamber in which he served.

Race prejudice is as old as the world, and as everlasting as the hills, and this prejudice—deep, uncircumscribed and uneradicable—sits like a shadow on the future of the weaker race. It makes the core of his problem, and it answers Council's earnest question with an inexorable "No!"

Under this prejudice the negro can never, North or South, be received in equal social and personal relations with the families of the white race, and can never, therefore, be a social equal with the white man.

Under this prejudice he will never, North or South, be permitted to govern in any State or country, even where he has a majority, and he can never, therefore, be a political equal.

If he can have, then, neither social nor political equality—and every fact and all theory and all instinct and every unbroken precedent declare that he can not—then he can never under these conditions reach the full development of a citizen or the full stature of a man. If he remains in this country, he must remain as an inferior, and his suffrage becomes a mockery and his liberty a farce.

It is a problem for the negro, because he can never compete with Anglo-Saxon civilization. Once more I recall that his is the weakest and ours the strongest race on earth. Our majority is 60,000,000, and we have a thousand years the start of him. No race has ever competed successfully with the Saxon, and where is the hope of the negro? In politics, in society, in industry and in trade there is no well-founded hope for the inferior race. History without a break, and precedent without a variation, proclaim this to be true. There is not a line of light or promise of equality for him in any field.

This is the core of my contention—the basis of my argument. All our splendid platitudes are wrecked on this stern fact. All our brave philanthropies beat out their beautiful lives on this inexorable truth. The negro fronts a hopeless and unequal competition!

There he stands, that helpless and unfortunate inferior. For his sake the one difference has widened between the sections of our common country. Over his black body we have shed rivers of blood and treasure to emphasize our separate convictions of his destiny. And yet, as the crimson tide rolls away into the years, we realize that all this blood and treasure and travail was spent in vain, and that the negro, whom a million Americans died to free, is in present bond and future promise still a slave, whipped by circumstance, trodden under foot by iron and ineradicable prejudice; shut out forever from the opportunities which are the heritage of liberty, and holding in his black hand the hollow parchment of his franchise as a free man, looks through a slave's eyes at the impassable barriers which imprison him forever within the progress and achievement of a dominant and all-conquering race.

By the whole unbroken record of Anglo-Saxon history, I swear that this is true.

Two things seem clear, then, in relation to the race problem. In its present status it compasses the progress of the white man with demoralization and difficulty that puts his very civilization in peril and disrepute.

In its present status it wraps the negro's destiny in unequal competition and leaves him helpless under the weight of a prejudice universal, unlifting, unchanging, and overwhelming.

Shall this experiment go on?

Will education soften these conditions and bring the experiment to success? Serious thinkers deeply question this. By the record of the census, the negro's criminality has increased as his illiteracy has decreased, and his race antagonism has grown with his intelligence. Education brings light, and light perception, and with quickened faculties the negro sees the difference between his real and his constitutional status in the republic. He sees that neither worth nor merit nor attainment can overcome the world-wide repulsion of type and color; and, seeing this, he is moved to rebellious protest and sometimes to violent revenge. Education spoils the laborer and makes inevitably, and logically, and laudably, the aspirant for social and political equalities which have been, and will be, forever denied him by the ruling race. Education develops wants which can not be supplied, and aspirations which never can be met. Industrial education will not win where mental education has failed. The hand is not greater than the head. Industrial competition will make a sterner struggle with the superior people. The battle of the loaf will be the deadliest and most destructive contest of the races.

Will the formal repeal of the Fifteenth Amendment cut the core from the political problem, and develop peace? I do not think so. The elimination of the negro from politics would remove him from strife and wrangle, and destroy the sectional bitterness with which his history has divided the republic. But it would cut hope and motive and ambition from his horizon, and leave him sunken and degraded, with nothing to live for but his creature comfort and his lust.

Will religion heal the problem and lose the prejudice of race in the brotherhood of man? Not this side of the millennium—not before the coming of Christ—will human nature undergo the regeneration that will bring this result to pass. If the spirit of Christ could pervade the world—if the devil of prejudice could be held in bondage for a thousand years—when the world is the new heaven; when man is everywhere the image of his Maker—these things may then be solved in the alembic of religion. But "ifs" are intangible, "whens" are immaterial, and both are millennial. For when these "ifs" are materialized into "is'es," and the "whens" are crystallized into "nows," then, indeed, this corruptible shall have put on incorruption, and this mortal shall have put on immortality in the land where prejudice is ended and problems have no place.

Can the strong race lift up the weaker to its level? Not in contact, not in proximity. Never. In the long, slow process the higher would inevitably sink nearer to the level of the lower race. Inferior races absorb the vices rather than the virtues of the superior race. The Hawaiian has degenerated in health and morals by contact with the English-speaking race. The Turanian and Tasmanian races perished by contact with higher civilization. The Maoris and New Zealanders suffered so, and the noble red man is to-day a besotted wretch perishing in the white heat of a civilization for which he was never designed. Not in equal relations, not side by side, can the higher race reform the lower. Apart and separate. by missionary and evangel, by example and by counsel, we may help an inferior race to be helpful, self-reliant, and free. But not under the shadow of our robust and stalwart sins, or under the iron weight of our all-conquering evils. History stamps discouragement on the theory everywhere.

May God keep this great Caucasian people from the poison of a "mongrel" blood!

Is there any other remedy? Is there any other balm in Gilead? Is there any healing here? Not within my vision, and not within the records of experience. Try all these remedies, test them all as they have all been tested and mocked in the trials of the years. Try any new remedy that wisdom or quackery may propose. And when we have tried them all, and have failed in all, as we are failing and will forever fail, it may be that Almighty God, the last imminent factor in the destiny of nations, will strike the scales from our blinded eyes and lead us by elimination and higher logic to see the remedy—the only remedy—His remedy.

For on the single occasion when the skies were parted for light upon the problem of the wrangling races, Almighty God reached down to Egypt and by the definite way of *separation*, led by the Jews, His chosen people, over seas of difficulty and through wildernesses of doubt to their promised land.

Separation of the races is the way—the only way. If God "hath made of one blood all the nations of the earth," He hath also "established unto them the metes and bounds of their habitation!" He did not intend that opposite and antagonistic races should live together. The prejudice of race is a pointing of providence, and the antagonism of peoples is the fixed policy by which God peoples the different portions of the universe and establishes the individuality of the nations. The act that brought these people together on this continent was a sin of the fathers—a sin of greed, an iniquity of trade—and the sorrow and suffering of the present is for the sin of the past, a sin against nature, and a sin against God. The curse can be lifted only when nature is vindicated and God is obeyed. The problem will be solved only when the negro is restored to the "bounds of his habitation."

The wisdom of our wise men has fallen in line with the wisdom of the Almighty. Some of the greatest names and greatest hearts in all our history have thought and said that *separation* was the logical, the inevitable, the only solution. Daniel Webster said so.

Thomas Jefferson said so, most definitely and eloquently. Edward Everett said so. James Madison said so. Henry Clay believed and said it. Twice in his glorious and illustrious lifetime, Abraham Lincoln, who did not believe in the negro as a citizen and a voter, moved in his public station toward a definite plan of *separation*. By the sending of Thomas Fortune to the Philippines, President Roosevelt is, inferentially at least, in consideration of a similar plan. Henry Grady believed in it. Bishop Turner is its open advocate. Blyden and Council and Taylor, and the ablest leaders of the race, are said to favor it; and I think that Booker Washington in his heart knows that neither worth nor merit nor achievement will ever bridge the impassable barrier of race prejudice, and that, when the last arrow of his noble but hopeless effort has been shot, it must come to this at last.

We have temporized for forty years upon this problem. In the exhaustion of all our expedients, in the failure of all our theories, and in the providence of God, we have come at last to the parting of the ways.

There is not a hope in fact or reason for the negro outside of separation.

There is no peace, no purity, no tranquil development, no durable prosperity, and no moral growth for the white race outside of separation.

It is neither impossible nor impracticable. The elements are willing and the way is in reach. This is not a day of impossibilities. To the genius, the energy, and the necessities of this age all things are possible. Every day sees the business world, the educational world, the political world converting the impossible into the possible. The hand of the Almighty is steadily opening the way.

It is a day of large things, a day of magnificent enterprises, a day of colossal movements everywhere.

England has offered a kingdom tract in Africa to the Jews of the world. The Zionist congress in Switzerland has met the offer, and the children of Israel—God's chosen people—scattered for centuries through all the world, will come trooping back to re-establish Israel as a nation and to make a New Jerusalem upon the earth. Wonderful and inspiring spectacle! Is there anything so wonderful, so marvelous, as this in the proposition to establish a compact, gregarious and comparatively docile race of negroes in a State or country of their own?

Is the expense appalling? Is the cost prohibitive? England again offers an example. England, our mother-country—England, next to ourselves, the greatest and most enlightened government under the sun—England has just put its hand into its pocket to expend $500,000,000 in order to buy out the Irish landlords and to heal the otherwise incurable running sore of Irish discontent. Wonderful liberality! Wonderful statesmanship!

We are as rich as England—richer than England, and twice as rich as any other kingdom in the world. We have as great a stake, as tremendous a necessity in this negro problem as England had with Ireland. We have already expended $1,000,000,000 in the futile effort to make the negro free. If England, just out of the war in Africa, can expend $500,000,000 to solve its Irish problem, then surely, the greatest of republics, in this era of peace and unparalleled prosperity—at the acme of its wealth, at the zenith of its greatness and power—can well afford to put a few hundred millions into the solution of the vital problem of its races—a problem demoralizing to one race and hopeless for another; a problem that menaces unity, purity and peace. Liberality in this emergency is superb economy.

The argument of analogy would seem conclusive. Somewhere, and in some way, if the races are to separate, there must be found a place for the negro, a plan of separation, an inducement, and the consent of the elements involved. Briefly and in fragmentary outline, let us consider these.

In the matter of location. Follow first the inferential line of the President of the United States—the Philippines. Thomas Fortune's mission was said to be successful. His report was published that the Philippine soil and climate was suited to the negro; that the territory was ample, and that on one of these islands he believed the fortunes of the negro and the native might be worked out side by side. It may be that the islands of the sea were placed by Providence in our keeping to furnish an answer to the problem of the times. The repatriation of Africa is the sentimental ideal of the advocates of separation—to go back to the Dark Continent from which they came, carrying the light, the law and the gospel of the great republic, after two centuries of touch, and side by side with the children of Israel, to establish anew the merits and the mission of an unfortunate race. If there be those who would oppose on philanthropic grounds the sending of the negro so far out of reach of help and regulation, there is land to be had at home. Lower California might be secured. The lands west of Texas might be had. But the government does not need to purchase. Four hundred million acres of government land is yet untaken and undeveloped in the West. Of these vast acres the expert hydrographer of the Interior Department has reported that it is easily possible to redeem by irrigation enough to support in plenty a population of sixty million people. So that the question of location is secure. A gregarious race might be settled anywhere within this scope of suggestion with a population not so dense as that of Belgium and the Netherlands. The cost would vary with the location, but under any conservative plan it would not be greater than England will spend in Ireland, and not nearly so much as the Jews for their New Jerusalem.

No reasonable or considerate plan would call for the wholesale or summary deportation of the negro. With his consent, and with governmental aid, the movement might proceed slowly and with consideration. The older negroes would scarcely care to go. They are passing rapidly to a land that our problems can not reach. Within conservative limits, the transportation even to Africa would be practicable and easy. If only the vessels that brought foreigners to our shores from 1880 to 1885 had carried back to Africa as many negroes as they brought immigrants to us, not a single black man, woman or child would have been left in the country in 1885! Carl McKinley, the ablest and clearest statistician who has ever figured on this line, has made it plain that to induce the annual emigration of 12,500 child-bearing females of the average age of twenty years, would remove the maternal element of the negro race in forty years, and leave it easy to carry the remaining part. To remove in forty years all the negroes who are now under the age of forty years, and to remove the increase only—all the children who shall be born within these forty years—would be the remainder of the problem—an easy and practicable task. And the same cool statistician, figuring liberally and counting it as sure that the government would do what it unquestionably ought to do, and send these people with some moneyed provision for their earlier wants, estimates that at $200 a head it would cost only $10,000,000 a year, which is less than one-twelfth of the nation's revenue from its internal taxes, or in forty years the total cost would be $400,000,000—or $100,000,000 less than England has just paid for peace and tranquility in Ireland. If any of you who hear should care to investigate this phase of the question deeply, and to carry these calculations forward, you will find Mr. McKinley's book, "An Appeal to Pharaoh," one of the most instructive and convincing volumes you have ever read.

Of course, in the event of locating the negro in this country, the cost would be largely but indefinitely reduced.

Whether a State or colony should be the form of government would be within the discretion of the statesmen who put this plan into action. If a State, it would have the model and example of our own States to shape its plan and government. It might be made a counterpart of our surrounding States; for the negro's is an imitative mind, and he could not find a nobler model. If a State, it should be exclusively a negro State. Every office in it, from chief justice of the court to coroner of the county, should be held exclusive to the negro race. Every white man should be debarred from right of franchise or of holding property in that State. It should be—especially if in this country—from first to last a negro State holding its rights under the Constitution—the right to representation in the Federal congress—paying its taxes to the government, but holding every right free and unchallenged, equal in every way to Illinois or Georgia. In the distribution of the army there might be placed a Federal garrison on its border for protection without and order within the State.

The superb inducement to the negro would be found in the freedom, the individuality, and the opportunity of an independent commonwealth, in which he would be freed from the unequal competition of a superior people, and given a chance to develop a character, and to demonstrate the merits of his leaders and the capacities of the race.

The constraining inducement to go should most unquestionably be given in an amendment to the Constitution which restricted his ballot to the State set apart for him by the generosity of the government. This would be fair. It would be equitable. Let no white man vote in the negro State to harass the negro councils, and let no negro vote in any other State than his own. Yon cannot vote in Georgia; I cannot vote in Illinois. The hardship is not great in view of the tremendous reasons that require it, and in return for the magnificent advantages which compensate it. This provision would be necessary as a controlling inducement for the change. Every aspiration in the negro race should set toward the state of his opportunity. And if, with this great goal before him, he hesitated to go, or failed in going, it would be the last crowning proof of the hopeless and remediless inferiority of his people. Never was proposition fairer. Never was compensation nobler to a race. A flag for a fetich; a country for a prison; and a glorious and unhindered opportunity for the empty mockery of a ballot, which has been and will be strangled here forever in his grasp.

Will the negro go? I think honestly and deliberately that he will. The protest of the very few well-fed, well-kept, and well-conditioned negroes who surround us here must not blind us to the plea of the helpless and hopeless thousands who see no light in the present and no hope in their future environment. Many of the ablest and truest leaders of the race are ardent advocates of separation. Bishop Turner, the wisest and most conservative leader of his race, is the advocate and evangel of a negro republic in Africa.

Ten thousand negroes in Kansas petitioned congress to appropriate money for a plan of separation. As a recognized advocate of the plan, I have had thousands of letters from negroes thanking me and bidding me God-speed with their prayers. Societies have been formed all over the country, some of them doing me the honor to bear my name, to organize the cooperative movement for a separate state. A circular carrying the plan was put ten years ago into the hands of one of the ablest and most eloquent negroes of the South. He carried it, not to persuade, but to explain to leading negroes in every section of the country, and out of 5,000 circulars 4,500 came back to us bearing the deliberate, grateful approval of the best representatives of the negro race. I believe that, fairly presented to his intelligence, fairly appealing to his love of change, and with a general understanding of its advantages and opportunities, the negro will thank God and bless America for a plan like this.

Will the white South be willing for the negro to go?

I frankly confess the promise of some opposition to the idea in the South. Paradoxical as it may seem, the South loves the negro—not the new negro, but the old. In his place and in the relations clearly understood, there is a feeling of affection between the southern white man and the better negroes which our friends to the north of us can never appreciate and never understand. But the relations of the races in the South are constantly growing more strained and unpleasant. The new negro is killing the relation established by the old negro. Every year the reluctance of the South to part with the negro is lessened, and the multiplying crimes and increasing unthrift of the negro are changing this reluctance to a positive anxiety for his departure.

The chief opposition in the South would rest upon

the misapprehension, which you doubtless share, that the negro is indispensable to the agriculture and labor conditions of that section. That was once true. It is no longer true. I state here for the first time a fact which will be as surprising to the South as it is to you: The negro no longer makes the staple or cereal crops of the South! The cotton of Texas, of Louisiana, and of Mississippi is made chiefly by the white man and not by the negro! The negro is no longer an industrial necessity. This fact is from the census. It is not as yet published, but it comes straight from an authority beyond question in the Labor Bureau at Washington. It is being verified and understood by the best observers and thinkers of the States; and when that fact—that tremendous fact, now so little understood—becomes generally known in the country and in the South, then the South will stand as solidly for separation as its humblest representative stands for it here to-day.

And if this means the reduction of our representation in Congress, let that come. It would be a temporary loss. The exodus of the negro will let in the tides of an improved and restricted immigration, and the working Swede, the thrifty German, and the gallant Irishman will come in to renew our political status and to fill the hiatus with a homogeneous people.

Will the northern white man be willing for the negro to go?

The politician, unthinking, and the philanthropist, far-thinking and generally over-thinking, answers, "No!" The masses—the real people—answer, "Yes!" Recent events have uncovered a revolution of sentiment in the North toward the negro. The masses have been disillusioned. The idleness, the ingratitude, the insolence, and the crime of the negro have alienated even his friends. Even the philanthropists must be hopeless at least over the unchanged and unchanging conditions which they protest. As for the politicians, they are parrots—echoes of opinions, which they follow, but never make. The masses, in some things at least, are the masters of the politicians—and the masses see the truth.

Standing here to-day, and standing as I have so often stood before the real people of the North and West, understanding their spirit and their temper, I announce before you, without hesitation and without reserve, that upon this issue and under the new light which the decade has brought it, I would be willing with absolute confidence to submit to the vote of the real people of the North and West the whole question of the South and the negro—whether that issue be disfranchisement or whether it be separation!

Let the negro continue to settle in the North, as he has done. And if the problem continues, it will be our only recourse to persuade him to settle in these great centers where our brethren may share and understand our perplexities. Let the tide continue to drift here—and the day will come when the laboring masses of the North will arise and demand a separation just as sternly as they demanded and secured the exclusion of the Chinese.

The philanthropist will grow weary, the theorist will despair, and the politician in time will undergo a change of heart. And we all shall come in the fulness of real philanthropy, and in the soundness of real discretion, to see the only solution—the one remedy—and to follow it in the fear of God and in the faith of the people, to prosperity and peace.

Ladies and gentlemen, my message is given and my mission is done. The scope of the discussion is too vast for an hour and too deep for a morning's thought. I have offered the bare elements which your brains and your scholarship must clothe with the form and substance of more elaborate truth. May the words which have been spoken in weakness be raised in strength, and may you see my people and their problem as you have not done before.

Let my parting words plead for the harmony and sympathy which lie for us beyond this dividing issue. Abraham Lincoln told you in 1859 that the Union "could not survive half slave and half free." I believe with all my mind that if he lived to-day his noble lips would frame again the truth that the Union cannot any longer live half black and half white—half slave and half free! This is an issue upon which it seems we can never agree.

For half a hundred years we have wrangled and fought and bled and died about this black man from Africa! Is the wrangle worth its fearful cost? Shall the great northern section of our common country always turn its hand against the great southern section of our country? Shall the young American of the North steel his heart against the young American of the South over an alien's cause? Shall the children of one blood and of a common glorious heritage divide in bitterness over a stranger in our midst? Shall the memories of Eutaw and Yorktown be obliterated in the recollections of Wilmington and Newnan? Shall the peace and harmony of this great republic be forever imperiled for the sake of the negro, whose faults and whose weakness so wonderfully outweigh his virtues and his gratitude? Shall the black man from Africa hinder and delay the work and the destiny of our imperial race?

Great God! The idea is monstrous and unthinkable! The South is neither cruel nor unpatriotic, and the North knows it. The North is neither immovable nor vindictive, and the South knows it. If either of us is mistaken, and if both of us are misunderstood, we are yet one people, and we must meet upon the plane of our brotherhood and our destiny.

Men and women of the University, I appeal to you who make the future. I appeal for Caucasian unity. I appeal for the imperial destiny of our mighty race. This is our country. We made it. We molded it. We control it, and we always will. We have done great things. We have mighty things yet to do. The negro is an accident—an unwilling, a blameless, but an unwholesome, unwelcome, helpless, unassimilable element in our civilization. He is not made for our times. He is not framed to share in the duty and the destiny which he perplexes and beclouds. Let us put him kindly and humanely out of the way. Let us give him a better chance than he has ever had in history, and let us have done with him. Let us solve his problem—frankly, fearlessly, nobly, and speedily. Let us put it behind us. Let us purify our politics of the perplexity. Let us liberate the South to vote and to think like free-men upon the mighty issues of the times.

And in the name of history and destiny, in the name of the past and in the name of the future, in the name of God and of our mission, I appeal to this great, conquering Caucasian race to lock arms and go forward and onward and upward to its essential work.

THE BOSTON BANQUET SPEECH.

By HENRY W. GRADY.

Mr. President: Bidden by your invitation to a discussion of the race problem—forbidden by occasion to make a political speech—I appreciate in trying to reconcile orders with propriety the predicament of the little maid who, bidden to learn to swim, was yet adjured, "Now, go, my darling, hang your clothes on a hickory limb, and don't go near the water."

The stoutest apostle of the church, they say, is the missionary, and the missionary, wherever he unfurls his flag, will never find himself in deeper need of unction and address than I, bidden to-night to plant the standard of a Southern Democrat in Boston's banquet-hall, and discuss the problem of the races in the home of Phillips and of Sumner. But, Mr. President, if a purpose to speak in perfect frankness and sincerity; if earnest understanding of the vast interests involved; if a consecrating sense of what disaster may follow further misunderstanding and estrangement, if these may be counted to steady undisciplined speech and to strengthen an untried arm—then, sir, I find the courage to proceed.

Happy am I that this mission has brought my feet at last to press New England's historic soil, and my eyes to the knowledge of her beauty and her thrift. Here, within touch of Plymouth Rock and Bunker Hill—where Webster thundered and Longfellow sang, Emerson thought and Channing preached—here in the cradle of American letters, and almost of American liberty, I hasten to make the obeisance that every American owes New England when first he stands uncovered in her mighty presence. Strange apparition! This stern and unique figure—carved from the ocean and the wilderness—its majesty kindling and growing amid the storms of winters and of wars—until at last the gloom was broken, its beauty disclosed in the sunshine, and the heroic workers rested at its base—while startled kings and emperors gazed and marveled that from the rude touch of this handful, cast on a bleak and unknown shore, should have come the embodied genius of human government, and the perfected model of human liberty! God bless the memory of those immortal workers—and prosper the fortunes of their living sons—and perpetuate the inspirations of their handiwork.

Two years ago, sir, I spoke some words in New York that caught the attention of the North. As I stand here to reiterate, as I have done everywhere, every word I then uttered—to declare that the sentiments I then avowed were universally approved in the South—I realize that the confidence begotten by that speech is largely responsible for my presence here to-night. I should dishonor myself if I betrayed that confidence by uttering one insincere word, or by withholding one essential element of the truth. Apropos of this last, let me confess, Mr. President—before the praise of New England has died on my lips—that I believe the best product of her present life is the procession of 17,000 Vermont Democrats that for twenty-two years, undiminished by death, unrecruited by birth or conversion, have marched over their rugged hills, cast their democratic ballots, and gone back home to pray for their unregenerate neighbors, and awake to read the record of 25,000 Republican majority. May God of the helpless and the heroic help them—and may their sturdy tribe increase!

Far to the south, Mr. President, separated from this section by a line, once defined in irrepressible difference, once traced in fraticidal blood,and now, thank God, but a vanishing shadow, lies the fairest and richest domain of this earth. It is the home of a brave and hospitable people. There, is centered all that can please or prosper humankind. A perfect climate, above a fertile soil, yields to the husbandman every product of the temperate zone. There, by night the cotton whitens beneath the stars, and by day the wheat locks the sunshine in its bearded sheaf. In the same field the clover steals the fragrance of the wind, and the tobacco catches the quick aroma of the rains. There, are mountains stored with exhaustless treasures; forests, vast and primeval, and rivers that, tumbling or loitering, run wanton to the sea. Of the three essential items of all industries—cotton, iron and wood—that region has easy control. In cotton, a fixed monopoly—in iron, proven supremacy—in timber, the reserve supply of the Republic. From this assured and permanent advantage, against which artificial conditions can not much longer prevail, has grown an amazing system of industries. Not maintained by human contrivance of tariff or capital, afar off from the fullest and cheapest source of supply, but resting in Divine assurance, within touch of field and mine and forest—not set amid costly farms from which competition has driven the farmer in despair, but amid cheap and sunny lands, rich with agriculture, to which neither season nor soil has set a limit—this system of industries is mounting to a splendor that shall dazzle and illumine the world.

That, sir, is the picture and the promise of my home —a land better and fairer than I have told you, and yet but fit setting, in its material excellence, for the loyal and gentle quality of its citizenship. Against that, sir, we have New England, recruiting the Republic from its sturdy loins, shaking from its overcrowded hives new swarms of workers and touching this land all over with its energy and its courage. And yet, while in the Eldorado of which I have told you, but 15 per cent. of lands are cultivated, its mines scarcely touched and its population so scant that, were it set equidistant, the sound of the human voice could not be heard from Virginia to Texas—while on the threshold of nearly every house in New England stands a son, seeking with troubled eyes some new land in which to carry his modest patrimony, the strange fact remains that in 1880 the South had fewer Northern-born citizens than she had in 1870—fewer in '70 than in '60. Why is this? Why is it, sir, though the sectional line be now but a mist that the breath may dispel, fewer men of the North have crossed it over to the South than when it was crimson with the best blood of the Republic, or even when the slaveholder stood guard every inch of its way?

There can be but one answer. It is the very problem we are now to consider. The key that opens that problem will unlock to the world the fairest half of this Republic, and free the halted feet of thousands whose eyes are already kindled with its beauty. Better than this, it will open the hearts of brothers for thirty years estranged, and clasp in lasting comradeship a million hands now withheld in doubt. Nothing, sir, but this problem, and the suspicions it breeds, hinders a clear understanding and a perfect union. Nothing else stands between us and such love as bound Georgia and Massachusetts at ValleyForge and Yorktown, chastened by the sacrifices at Manasses and Gettysburg, and illumined with the coming of better work and a nobler destiny than was ever wrought with the sword or sought at the cannon's mouth.

If this does not invite your patient hearing to-night —hear one thing more. My people, your brothers in the South—brothers in blood, in destiny, in all that is best in our past and future—are so beset with this problem that their very existence depends upon its right solution. Nor are they wholly to blame for its presence. The slave-ships of the Republic sailed from your ports—the slaves worked in our fields. You will not defend the traffic, nor I the institution. But I do hereby declare that in its wise and human administration, in lifting the slave to heights of which he had not dreamed in his savage home, and giving him a happiness he has not yet found in freedom—our fathers left their sons a saving and excellent heritage. In the storm of war this institution was lost. I thank God as heartily as you do that human slavery is gone forever from the American soil. But the freedman remains. With him a problem without precedent or parallel. Note its appalling conditions. Two utterly dissimilar races on the same soil—with equal political and civil rights—almost equal in numbers, but terribly unequal in intelligence and responsibility—each pledged against fusion—one for a century in servitude to the other, and freed at last by a desolating war —the experiment sought by neither, but approached by both with doubt—these are the conditions. Under these, adverse at every point, we are required to carry these two races in peace and honor to the end. Never, sir, has such a task been given to mortal stewardship. Never before in this Republic has the white race divided on the rights of an alien race. The red man was cut down as a weed, because he hindered the way of the American citizen. The yellow man was shut out of this Republic because he is an alien and inferior. The red man was owner of the land—the yellow man highly civilized and assimilable—but they hindered both sections and are gone! But the black man, affecting but one section, is clothed with every privilege of government and pinned to the soil, and my people commended to make good at any hazard, and at any cost, his full and equal heirship of American privilege and prosperity. It matters not that wherever the whites and blacks have touched, in any era, or any clime, there has been irreconcilable violence. It matters not that no two races, however similar, have lived anywhere at any time on the same soil with equal rights in peace! In spite of these things, we are commanded to make good this change of American policy which has not perhaps changed American prejudice—to make certain here what has elsewhere been impossible between whites and blacks—and to reverse, under the very worst conditions, the universal verdict of racial history. And driven, sir, to this superhuman task with an impatience that brooks no delay—a rigor that accepts no excuse—and a suspicion that discourages frankness and sincerity. We do not shrink from this trial. It is so interwoven with our industrial fabric that we can not disentangle it if we would—so bound up in our honorable obligation to the world, that we would not, if we could. Can we solve it? The God who gave it into our hands, He alone can know. But this the weakest and wisest of us do know: we can not solve it with less than your tolerant and patient sympathy—with less than the knowledge that the blood that runs in your veins is our blood—and that when we have done our best, whether the issue be lost or won, we shall feel your strong arms about us and hear the beating of your approving hearts.

The resolute, clear-headed, broad-minded men of the South—the men whose genius made glorious every page of the first seventy years of American history—whose courage and fortitude you tested in five years of the fiercest war—whose energy has made bricks without straw, and spread splendor amid the ashes of their war-wasted homes—these men wear this problem in their hearts and their brains, by day and by night. They realize, as you can not, what this problem means—what they owe to this kindly and dependent race—the measure of their debt to the world in whose despite they defended and maintained slavery. And though their feet are hindered in its undergrowth, and their march encumbered with its burdens, they have lost neither the patience from which comes clearness, nor the faith from which comes courage. Nor, sir, when in passionate moments is disclosed to them that vague and awful shadow, with its lurid abysses and its crimson stains, into which I pray God they may never go, are they struck with more of apprehension than is needed to complete their consecration!

Such is the temper of my people. But what of the problem itself? Mr. President, we need not go one step further unless you concede right here the people I speak for are as honest, as sensible, and as just as your people, seeking as earnestly as you would in their place, to rightly solve the problem that touches them at every vital point. If you insist that they are ruffians, blindly striving with bludgeon and shotgun to plunder and oppress a race, then I shall sacrifice my self-respect and tax your patience in vain. But admit that they are men of common sense and common honesty—wisely modifying an environment they can not wholly disregard—guiding and controlling as best they can the vicious and irresponsible of either race—

compensating error with frankness, and retrieving in patience what they lose in passion—and conscious all the time that wrong means ruin—admit this, and we may reach an understanding to-night.

The President of the United States, in his late message to Congress, discussing the plea that the South should be left to solve this problem, asks: "Are they at work upon it? What solution do they offer? When will the black man cast a free ballot? When will he have the civil rights that are his?" I shall not here protest against the partisanry that, for the first time in our history, in time of peace, has stamped with the great seal of our government a stigma upon the people of a great and loyal section, though I gratefully remember that the great dead soldier, who held the helm of state for the eight stormy years of reconstruction, never found need for such a step; and though there is no personal sacrifice I would not make to remove this cruel and unjust imputation on my people from the archives of my country! But, sir, backed by a record, on every page of which is progress, I venture to make earnest and respectful answer to the questions that are asked. I bespeak your patience, while, with vigorous plainness of speech, seeking your judgment rather than your applause, I proceed, step by step. We give to the world this year a crop of 7,500,000 bales of cotton, worth $45,000,000, and its cash equivalent in grain, grasses and fruit. This enorumous crop could not have come from the hands of sullen and discontented labor. It comes from peaceful fields, in which laughter and gossip rise above the hum of industry, and contentment runs with the singing plow.

It is claimed that this ignorant labor is defrauded of its just hire. I present the tax books of Georgia, which show that the negro, twenty-five years ago a slave, has in Georgia alone, $10,000,000 of assessed property, worth twice that much. Does not that record honor him, and vindicate his neighbors? What people, penniless, illiterate, has done so well? For every Afro-American agitator, stirring the strife in which alone he prospers, I can show you a thousand negroes, happy in their cabin homes, tilling their own land by day, and at night taking from the lips of their children the helpful message their State sends them from the schoolhouse door. And the schoolhouse itself bears testimony. In Georgia we added last year $250,000 to the school fund, making a total of more than $1,000,000—and this in the face of prejudice not yet conquered—of the fact that the whites are assessed for $368,000,000, the blacks for $10,000,000, and yet forty-nine per cent. of the beneficiaries are black children—and in the doubt of many wise men if education helps, or can help, our problem. Charleston, with her taxable values cut half in two since 1860, pays more in proportion for public schools than Boston. Although it is easier to give much out of much than little out of little, the South, with one-seventh of the taxable property of the country, with relatively larger debt, having received only one-twelfth as much public land, and having back of its tax-books none of the half billion of bonds that enrich the North—and though it pays annually $26,000,000 to your section as pensions, yet gives nearly one-sixth of the public school fund. The South, since 1865, has spent $122,000,000 in education, and this year is pledged to $37,000,000 for State and city schools, although the blacks, paying one-thirtieth of the taxes, get nearly one-half of the fund.

Go into our fields and see whites and blacks working side by side. On our buildings in the same squad. In our shops at the same forge. Often the blacks crowd the whites from work, or lower wages by the greater need or simpler habits, and yet are permitted because we want to bar them from no avenue in which their feet are fitted to tread. They could not there be elected orators of the white universities, as they have been here, but they do enter there a hundred useful trades that are closed against them here. We hold it better and wiser to tend the weeds in the garden than to water the exotic in the window. In the South, there are negro lawyers, teachers, editors, dentists, doctors, preachers, multiplying with the increasing ability of their race to support them. In villages and towns they have their military companies equipped from the armories of the State, their churches and societies built and supported largely by their neighbors. What is the testimony of the courts In penal legislation we have steadily reduced felonies to misdemeanors, and have led the world in mitigating punishment for crime, that we might save, as far as possible, this dependent race from its own weakness. In our penitentiary record sixty per cent. of the prosecutors are negroes, and in every court the negro criminal strikes the colored juror, that white men may judge his case. In the North, one negro in every 1,865 is in jail—in the South only one in 446. In the North the percentage of negro prisoners is six times as great as native whites—in the South, only four times as great. If prejudice wrongs him in Southern courts, the record shows it to be deeper in Northern courts.

I assert here, and a bar as intelligent and upright as the bar of Massachusetts will solemnly indorse my assertion, that in the Southern courts, from highest to lowest, pleading for life, liberty or property, the negro has distinct advantage because he is a negro, apt to be overreached, oppressed—and that this advantage reaches from the juror in making his verdict to the judge in measuring his sentence. Now, Mr. President, can it be seriously maintained that we are terrorizing the people from whose willing hands come every year $1,000,000,000 of farm crops? Or have robbed a people who, twenty-five years from unrewarded slavery have amassed in one State $20,000,000 of property? Or that we intend to oppress the people we are arming every day? Or deceive them when we are educating them to the utmost limit of our ability? Or outlaw them when we work side by side with them? Or re-enslave them under legal forms when for their benefit we have even imprudently narrowed the limit of felonies and mitigated the severity of law? My fellow countrymen, as you yourself may sometimes have to appeal to the bar of human judgment for justice and for right, give to my people to-night the fair and unanswerable conclusion of these incontestible facts.

But it is claimed that under this fair seeming there is disorder and violence. This I admit. And there will be until there is one ideal community on earth after which we may pattern. But how widely it is misjudged! It is hard to measure with exactness whatever touches the negro. His helplessness, his isolation, his century of servitude, these dispose us to emphasize and magnify his wrongs. This disposition, inflamed by prejudice and partisanry, has led to injustice and delusion. Lawless men may ravage a county in Iowa and it is accepted as an incident—in the South a drunken row is declared to be the fixed habit of the community. Regulators may whip vagabonds in Indiana by platoons, and it scarcely arrests attention—a chance collision in the South among relatively the same classes is gravely accepted as evidence that one race is destroying the other. We might as well claim that the Union was ungrateful to the colored soldiers who followed its flag, because a Grand Army post in Connecticut closed its doors to a negro veteran, as for you to give racial significance to every incident in the South, or to accept exceptional grounds as the rule of our society. I am not one of those who becloud American honor with the parade of the outrages of either section, and belie American character by declaring them to be significant and representative. I prefer to maintain that they are neither, and stand for nothing but the passion and the sin of our poor fallen humanity. If society, like a machine, were no stronger than its weakest part, I should despair of both sections. But, knowing that society, sentient and responsible in every fibre, can mend and repair until the whole has the strength of the best, I despair of neither. These gentlemen who come with me here, knit into Georgia's busy life as they are, never saw, I dare assert, an outrage committed on a negro! And if they did, not one of you would be swifter to prevent or punish. It is through them, and the man who thinks with them—making nine-tenths of every Southern community—that these two races have been carried thus far with less of violence than would have been possible anywhere else on earth. And in their fairness and courage and steadfastness—more than in all the laws that can be passed, or all the bayonets that can be mustered—is the hope of our future.

When will the black cast a free ballot? When ignorance anywhere is not dominated by the will of the intelligent; when the laborer anywhere casts a vote unhindered by his boss; when the vote of the poor anywhere is not influenced by the power of the rich; when the strong and the steadfast do not everywhere control the suffrage of the weak and shiftless—then, and not till then, will the ballot of the negro be free. The white people of the South are banded, Mr. President, not in prejudice against the blacks—not in sectional estrangement, not in the hope of political dominion, but in a deep and abiding necessity. Here is this vast ignorant and purchasable vote—clannish, credulous, impulsive and passionate—tempting every art of the demagogue, but insensible to the appeal of the statesman. Wrongly started, in that it was led into alienation from its neighbor and taught to rely on the protection of an outside force, it can not be merged and lost in the two great parties through logical currents, for it lacks political conviction and even that information on which conviction must be based. It must remain a faction—strong enough in every community to control on the slightest division of the whites. Under that division it becomes the prey of the cunning and unscrupulous of both parties. Its credulity is imposed on, its patience inflamed, its cupidity tempted, its impulses misdirected—and even its superstition made to play its part in a campaign in which every interest of society is jeopardized and every approach to the ballot-box debauched. It is against such campaigns as this—the folly and the bitterness and the danger of which every Southern community has drunk deeply—that the white people of the South are banded together. Just as you in Massachusetts would be banded if 300,000 black men—not one in a hundred able to read his ballot—banded in a race instinct, holding against you the memory of a century of slavery, taught by your late conquerors to distrust and oppose you, had already travestied legislation from your statehouse, and in every species of folly or villainy has wasted your substance and exhausted your credit.

But admitting the right of the whites to unite

against this tremendous menace, we are challenged with the smallness of our vote. This has long been flippantly charged to the evidence, and has now been solemnly and officially declared to be proof of political turpitude and baseness on our part. Let us see. Virginia—a State now under fierce assault for this alleged crime—cast, in 1888, seventy-five per cent. of her vote. Was it suppression in Virginia and natural causes in Massachusetts? Last month Virginia cast sixty-nine per cent. of her vote, and Massachusetts, fighting in every district, cast only forty-six per cent. of hers. If Virginia is condemned because thirty-one per cent. of her vote was silent, how shall this State escape in which fifty-one per cent. was dumb? Let us enlarge this comparison. The sixteen Southern States in 1888 cast sixty-seven per cent. of their total vote—the six New England States but sixty-three per cent. of theirs. By what fair rule shall the stigma be put upon one section, while the other escapes? A congressional election in New York last week, with the polling-place within touch of every voter, brought out only 6,000 votes of 28,000—and the lack of opposition is assigned as the natural cause. In a district in my State, in which an opposition speech has not been heard in ten years, and the polling-places are miles apart—under the unfair reasoning of which my section has been a constant victim—the small vote is charged to be proof of forcible suppression. In Virginia an average majority of 10,000, under hopeless division of the minority, was raised to 42,000; in Iowa, in the same election, a majority of 32,000 was wiped out, and an opposition majority of 8,000 was established. The change of 42,000 votes in Iowa is accepted as political revolution—in Virginia an increase of 30,000 on a safe majority is declared to be proof of political fraud. I charge these facts and figures home, sir, to the heart and conscience of the American people, who will not assuredly see one section condemned for what another section is excused!

If I can drive them through the prejudice of the partisan, and have them read and pondered at the fireside of the citizen, I will rest on the judgment there formed and the verdict there rendered!

It is deplorable, sir, that in both sections a larger percentage of the vote is not regularly cast, but more inexplicable that this should be so in New England than in the South. What invites the negro to the ballot-box? He knows that, of all men, it has promised him most and yielded him least. His first appeal to suffrage was the promise of "forty acres and a mule." His second, the threat that Democratic success meant his re-enslavement. Both have proved false in his experience. He looked for a home, and he got the Freedman's Bank. He fought under the promise of the loaf, and in victory was denied the crumbs. Discouraged and deceived, he has realized at last that his best friends are his neighbors, with whom his lot is cast, and whose prosperity is bound up in his—and that he has gained nothing in politics to compensate the loss of their confidence and sympathy that is at last his best and his enduring hope. And so, without leaders or organization—and lacking the resolute heroism of my party friends in Vermont, that makes their hopeless march over the hills a high and inspiring pilgrimage—he shrewdly measures the occasional agitator, balances his little account with politics, touches up his mule and jogs down the furrow, letting the mad world jog as it will!

The negro vote can never control in the South, and it would be well if partisans in the North would understand this. I have seen the white people of a State set about by black hosts until their fate seemed sealed.

But, sir, some brave man, banding them together, would rise, as Elijah rose in beleagured Samaria, and, touching their eyes with faith, bid them look abroad to see the very air "filled with the chariots of Israel and the horsemen thereof." If there is any human force that can not be withstood, it is the power of the banded intelligence and responsibility of a free community. Against it, numbers and corruption can not prevail. It can not be forbidden in the law or divorced in force. It is the inalienable right of every free community—and the just and righteous safeguard against an ignorant or corrupt suffrage. It is on this, sir, that we rely in the South. Not the cowardly menace of mask or shotgun, but the peaceful majesty of intelligence and responsibility, massed and unified for the protection of its homes and the preservation of its homes and the preservation of its liberty. That, sir, is our reliance and our hope, and against it all the powers of the earth shall not prevail. It was just as certain that Virginia would come back to the unchallenged control of her white race—that before the moral and material power of her people once more unified, opposition would crumble until its last desperate leader was left alone vainly striving to rally his disordered hosts—as that night should fade in the kindling glory of the sun. You may pass force bills, but they will not avail. You may surrender your liberties to Federal election law, you may submit, in fear of a necessity that does not exist, that the very form of this government may be changed—this old State that holds in its charter the boast that "it is a free and independent commonwealth"—it may deliver its election machinery into the hands of the government it helped to create—but never, sir, will a single State in this Union, North or South, be delivered again to the control of an ignorant and inferior race.

We wrested our State government from negro supremacy when the Federal drumbeat rolled closer to the ballot-box and Federal bayonets hedged it deeper about than will ever again be permitted in this free government. But, sir, though the cannon of this Republic thundered in every voting district of the South, we still should find in the mercy of God the means and the courage to prevent its re-establishment!

I regret, sir, that my section, hindered with this problem, stands in seeming estrangement to the North. If, sir, any man will point out to me a path down which the white people of the South divided may walk in peace and honor, I will take that path though I took it alone—for at the end, and nowhere else, I fear, is to be found the full prosperity of my section and the full restoration of this Union. But, sir, if the negro had not been enfranchised, the South would have been divided and the Republic holds the South united and compact. What solution, then, can we offer for this problem? Time alone can disclose it to us. We simply report progress and ask your patience. If the problem be solved at all—and I firmly believe it will, though nowhere else has it been—it will be solved by the people most deeply bound in interest, most deeply pledged in honor to its solution. I had rather see my people render back this question rightly solved than to see them gather all the spoils over which faction has contended since Catiline conspired and Caesar fought. Meantime we treat the negro fairly, measuring to him justice in the fullness the strong should give to the weak, and leading him in the steadfast ways of citizenship that he may no longer be the prey of the unscrupulous and the sport of the thoughtless. We open to him every pursuit in which he can prosper, and seek to broaden his training and capacity. We seek to hold his confidence and friendship, and to pin him to the soil with ownership, that he may catch in the fire of his own hearthstone that sense of responsibility the shiftless can never know. And we gather him into that alliance of intelligence and responsibility that, though it now runs close to racial lines, welcomes the responsible and intelligent of any race. By this course, confirmed in our judgment and justified in the progress already made, we hope to progress slowly but surely to the end.

The love we feel for that race you can not measure nor comprehend. As I attest it here, the spirit of my old black mammy from her home up there looks down to bless, and through the tumult of this night steals the sweet music of her crooning as thirty years ago she held me in her black arms and led me smiling into sleep. This scene vanishes as I speak, and I catch a vision of an old Southern home, with its lofty pillars, and its white pigeons fluttering down through the golden air. I see women with strained and anxious faces, and children alert, yet helpless. I see night come down with its dangers and its apprehensions, and in a big homely room I feel on my tired head the touch of loving hands—now worn and wrinkled, but fairer to me yet than the hands of mortal woman, and stronger yet to lead me than the hands of mortal man—as they lay a mother's blessing there while at her knees—the truest altar I yet have found—I thank God that she is safe in her sanctuary, because her slaves, sentinel in the silent cabin or guard at her chamber door, puts a black man's loyalty between her and danger.

I catch another vision. The crisis of battle—a soldier struck, staggering, fallen. I see a slave, scuffling through the smoke, winding his black arms about the fallen form, reckless of the hurtling death—bending his trusty face to catch the words that tremble on the stricken lips, so wrestling meantime with agony that he would lay down his life in his master's stead. I see him by the weary bedside, ministering with uncomplaining patience, praying with all his humble heart that God will lift his master up, until death come in mercy and in honor to still the soldier's agony and seal the soldier's life. I see him by the open grave, mute, motionless, uncovered, suffering for the death of him who in life fought against his freedom. I see him when the mound is heaped and the great drama of his life is closed, turn away, and with downcast eyes and uncertain step start out into new and strange fields, faltering, struggling, but moving on, until his shambling figure is lost in the light of this better and brighter day. And from the grave comes a voice saying: "Follow him! Put your arms about him in his need, even as he put his about me. Be his friend as he was mine." And out into this new world—strange to me as to him, dazzling, bewildering both—I follow! And may God forget my people—when they forget these.

Whatever the future may hold for them—whether they plod along in the servitude from which they have never been lifted since the Cyrenian was laid hold upon by the Roman soldiers and made to bear the cross of the fainting Christ—whether they find homes again in Africa, and thus hasten the prophecy of the psalmist who said: "And suddenly Ethiopia shall hold out her hands unto God"—whether forever dislocated and separated, they remain a weak people beset by stronger, and exist as the Turk, who lives in the jealousy rather than in the conscience of Europe—or whether in this miraculous Repubic they break through the caste of twenty centuries and, belying universal history, reach the full stature of citizenship, and in peace maintain it—we shall give them uttermost justice and abiding friendship. And whatever we do, into whatever seeming estrangement we may be driven, nothing shall disturb the love we bear this Republic, or mitigate our consecration to its service. I stand here, Mr. President, to profess no new loyalty. When General Lee, whose heart was the temple of our hopes, and whose arm was clothed with our strength, renewed his allegiance to the government at Appomattox, he spoke from a heart too great to be false, and he spoke for every honest man from Maryland to Texas. From that day to this, Hamilcar has nowhere in the South sworn young Hannibal to hatred and vengeance—but everywhere to loyalty and to love. Witness the soldier standing at the base of a Confederate monument above the graves of his comrades, his empty sleeve tossing in the April wind, adjuring the young men about him to serve as honest and loyal citizens the government against which their fathers fought. This message, delivered from that sacred presence, has gone home to the hearts of my fellows! And, sir, I declare here, if physical courage be always equal to human aspiration, that they would die, sir, if need be, to restore this Republic their fathers fought to dissolve!

Such, Mr. President, is this problem, as we see it; such is the temper in which we approach it; such the progress made. What do we ask of you? First, patience; out of this alone can come perfect work. Second, confidence; in this alone can you judge fairly. Third, sympathy; in this you can help us best. Fourth, give us your sons as hostages. When you plant your capital in millions, send your sons that they may help know how true are our hearts and may help to swell the Anglo-Saxon current until it can carry without danger this black infusion. Fifth, loyalty to the Republic—for there is sectionalism in loyalty as in estrangement. This hour little needs the loyalty that is loyal to one section and yet holds the other in enduring suspicion and estrangement. Give us the broad and perfect loyalty that loves and trusts Georgia alike with Massachusetts—that knows no South, no North, no East, no West; but endears with equal and patriotic love every foot of our soil, every State of our Union.

A mighty duty, sir, and a mighty inspiration impels every one of us to-night to lose in patriotic consecration whatever estranges, whatever divides. We, sir, are Americans—and we fight for human liberty. The uplifting force of the American idea is under every throne on earth. France, Brazil—these are our victories. To redeem the earth from kingcraft and oppression—this is our mission. And we shall not fail. God has sown in our soil the seed of his millennial harvest, and he will not lay the sickle to the ripening crop until his full and perfect day has come. Our history, sir, has been a constant and expanding miracle from Plymouth Rock and Jamestown all the way—aye, even from the hour when, from the voiceless and trackless ocean, a new world rose to the sight of the inspired sailor. As we approach the fourth centennial of that stupendous day—when the old world will come to marvel and to learn, amid our gathered treasures—let us resolve to crown the miracles of our past with the spectacle of a republic compact, united, indissoluble in the bonds of love—loving from the Lakes to the Gulf—the wounds of war healed in every heart as on every hill—serene and resplendent at the summit of human achievement and earthly glory—blazing out the path, and making clear the way up which all the nations of the earth must come in God's appointed time!

BUT WHAT OF THE NEGRO.

EXCERPTS FROM THE NEW SOUTH SPEECH DELIVERED BY HENRY W. GRADY AT THE BANQUET OF THE NEW ENGLAND CLUB, NEW YORK.

It is a rare privilege, sir, to have had part, however humble, in this work. Never was nobler duty confided to human hands than the uplifting and upbuilding of the prostrate and bleeding South—misguided, perhaps, but beautiful in her suffering, and honest, brave and generous always. In the record of her social, industrial and political illustration we await with confidence the verdict of the world.

Have we solved the problem he presents or progressed in honor and equity toward solution? Let the record speak to the point. No section shows a more prosperous laboring population than the negroes of the South, none in fuller sympathy with the employing and land-owning class. He shares our school fund, has the fullest protection of our laws and the friendship of our people. Self-interest, as well as honor, demand that he should have this. Our future our very existence depend upon our working out this problem in full and exact justice. We understand that when Lincoln signed the emancipation proclamation, your victory was assured, for he then committed you to the cause of human liberty, against which the arms of man can not prevail—while those of our statesmen who trusted to make slavery the cornerstone of the Confederacy doomed us to defeat as far as they could, committing us to a cause that reason could not defend or the sword maintain in sight of advancing civilization.

Had Mr. Toombs said, which he did not say, "that he would call the roll of his slaves at the foot of Bunker Hill," he would have been foolish, for he might have known that whenever slavery became entangled in war it must perish, and that the chattel in human flesh ended forever in New England when your fathers—not to be blamed for parting with what didn't pay—sold their slaves to our fathers—not to be praised for knowing a paying thing when they saw it. The relations of the Southern people with the negro are close and cordial. We remember with what fidelity for four years he guarded our defenseless women and children, whose husbands and fathers were fighting against his freedom. To his eternal credit be it said that whenever he struck a blow for his own liberty he fought in open battle, and when at last he raised his black and humble hands that the shackles might be struck off, those hands were innocent of wrong against his helpless charges, and worthy to be taken in loving grasp by every man who honors loyalty and devotion. Ruffians have maltreated him, rascals have misled him, philanthropists established a bank for him, but the South, with the North, protests against injustice to this simple and sincere people. To liberty and enfranchisement is as far as law can carry the negro. The rest must be left to the conscience and common sense. It must be left to those among whom his lot is cast, with whom he is indissolubly connected, and whose prosperity depends upon their possessing his intelligent sympathy and confidence. Faith has been kept with him, in spite of calumnious assertions to the contrary by those who assume to speak for us or by frank opponents. Faith will be kept with him in the future, if the South hold her reason and integrity.

But have we kept our faith with you? In the fullest sense, yes. When Lee surrendered—I don't say when Johnson surrendered, because I understand he still alludes to the time when he met General Sherman last as the time when he determined to abándon any further prosecution of the struggle—when Lee surrendered, I say, and Johnson quit, the South became, and has since been, loyal to this Union. We fought hard enough to know that we were whipped, and in perfect frankness accept as final the arbitrament of the sword to which we had appealed. The South found her jewel in the toad's head of defeat. The shackles that had held her in narrow limitations fell forever when the shackles of the negro slave were broken. Under the old regime the negroes were slaves to the South; the South was a slave to the system. The old plantation, with its simple police regulations and feudal habit, was the only type possible under slavery. Thus was gathered in the hands of a splendid and chivalric oligarchy the substance that should have been diffused among the people, as the rich blood, under certain artificial conditions, is gathered at the heart, filling that with affluent rapture but leaving the body chill and colorless.

WHAT OF THE NEGRO.

EXCERPTS FROM "THE SOUTH AND HER PROBLEMS," DELIVERED AT THE DALLAS STATE FAIR BY HENRY W. GRADY.

This of him. I want no better friend than the black boy who was raised by my side, and who is now trudging patiently with downcast eyes and shambling figure through his lowly way in life. I want no sweeter music than the crooning of my old "mammy," now dead and gone to rest, as I heard it when she held me in her loving arms, and bending her old black face above me stole the cares from my brain, and led me smiling into sleep. I want no truer soul than that which moved the trusty slave, who for four years while my father fought with the armies that barred his freedom, slept every night at my mother's chamber door, holding her and her children as safe as if her husband stood guard, and ready to lay down his humble life on her threshold. History has no parallel to the faith kept by the negro in the South during the war. Often five hundred negroes to a single white man, and yet through these dusky throngs the women and children walked in safety, and the unprotected homes rested in peace. Unmarshaled the black battalions moved patiently to the fields in the morning to feed the armies their idleness would have starved, and at night gathered anxiously at the big house to "hear the news from marster," though conscious that his victory made their chains enduring. Everywhere humble and kindly; the bodyguard of the helpless; the rough companion of the little ones; the observant friend; the silent sentry in his lowly cabin; the shrewd counsellor. And when the dead came home, a mourner at the open grave. A thousand torches would have disbanded every Southern army, but not one was lighted. When the master going to a war in which slavery was involved said to his slave, "I leave my home and loved ones in your charge," the tenderness between man and master stood disclosed. And when the slave held that charge sacred through storm and temptation, he gave new meaning to faith and loyalty. I rejoice that when freedom came to him after years of waiting, it was all the sweeter because the black hands from which the shackles fell were stainless of a single crime against the helpless ones confided to his care.

From this root, imbedded in a century of kind and constant companionship, has sprung some foliage. As no race had ever lived in such unresisting bondage, none was ever heard with such swiftness through freedom into power. Into hands still trembling from the blow that broke the shackles, was thrust the ballot. In less than twelve months from the day he walked down the furrow a slave, the negro dictated in legislative halls from which Davis and Calhoun had gone forth, the policy of twelve commonwealths. When his late master protested against his misrule, the federal drum-beat rolled around his strongholds, and from a hedge of federal bayonets he grinned in good-natured insolence. From the proven incapacity of that day has he far advanced? Simple, credulous, impulsive—easily led and too often easily bought, is he a safer, more intelligent citizen now than then? Is this mass of votes, loosed from old restraints, inviting alliance or awaiting opportunity, less menacing than when its purpose was plain and its way direct?

My countrymen, right here the South must make a decision on which very much depends. Many wise men hold that the white vote of the South should divide, the color line be beaten down, and the Southern States ranged on economic or moral questions as interest or belief demands. I am compelled to dissent from this view. The worst thing, in my opinion, that could happen is that the white people of the South should stand in opposing factions, with the vast mass of ignorant or purchasable negro votes between. Consider such a status. If the negroes were skillfully led—and leaders would not be lacking—it would give them the balance of power—a thing not to be considered. If their vote was not compacted, it would invite the debauching bid of factions, and drift surely to that which was the most corrupt and cunning. With the shiftless habit and irresolution of slavery days still possessing him, the negro voter will not in this generation, adrift from war issues, become a steadfast partisan through conscience or conviction. In every community there are colored men who redeem their race from this reproach, and who vote under reason. Perhaps in time the bulk of this race may thus adjust itself. But, through what long and monstrous periods of political debauchery this status would be reached, no tongue can tell.

The clear and unmistakable domination of the white race, dominating not through violence, not through party alliance, but through the integrity of its own vote and the largeness of its sympathy and justice through which it shall compel the support of the better classes of the colored race—that is the hope and assurance of the South. Otherwise, the negro would be bandied from one faction to another. His credulity would be played upon, his cupidity tempted, his impulses misdirected, his passions inflamed. He would be forever in alliance with that faction which was most desperate and unscrupulous. Such a state would be worse than reconstruction, for then intelligence was banded, and its speedy triumph assured. But with intelligence and property divided—bidding and overbidding for place and patronage—irritation increasing with each conflict—the bitterness and desperation seizing every heart—political debauchery deepening, as each faction staked its all in the miserable game—there would be no end in this, until our suffrage was hopelessly sullied, our people forever divided, and our most sacred rights surrendered.

One thing further should be said in perfect frankness. Up to this point we have dealt with ignorance and corruption—but beyond this point a deeper issue confronts us. Ignorance may struggle to enlightenment, out of corruption may come the incorruptible. God speed the day when—every true man will work and pray for its coming—the negro must be led to know and through sympathy to confess that his interests and the interests of the people of the South are identical. The men who, from afar off, view this subject through the cold eye of speculation or see it distorted through partisan control of the affairs of the South. We have no fears of this; already we are attaching to us the best elements of the race, and as we proceed our alliance will broaden; eternal pressure but irritates and impedes. Those who would put the negro race in supremacy would work against infallible decree, for the white race can never submit to its domination, because the white race is the superior race. But the supremacy of the white race of the South must be maintained forever, and the domination of the negro race resisted at all points and at all hazards—because the white race is the superior race. This is the declaration of no new truth. It has abided forever in the marrow of our bones, and shall run forever with the blood that feeds Anglo-Saxon hearts.

In political compliance the South has evaded the truth, and men have drifted from their convictions. But we can not escape this issue. It faces us wherever we turn. It is an issue that has been, and will be. The races and tribes of earth are of divine origin. Behind the laws of man and the decrees of war, stands the law of God. What God hath separated let no man join together. The Indian, the Malay, the Negro, the Caucasian, these types stand as markers of God's will. Let no man tinker with the work of the Almighty. Unity of civilization, no more than unity of faith, will never be witnessed on earth. No race has risen, or will rise, above the ordinary place. Here is the pivotal fact of this great matter—two races are made equal in law, and in political rights, between whom the caste of race has set an impassable gulf. This gulf is bridged by a statute, and the races are urged to cross thereon. This can not be. The fiat of the Almighty has gone forth, and in eighteen centuries of history, it is written. We would escape this issue if we could. From the depths of its soul the South invokes from heaven "peace on earth, and good will to man." She would not, if she could, cast this race back into the condition from which it was righteously raised. She would not deny its smallest or abridge its fullest privilege. Not to lift this burden forever from her people would she do the least of these things. She must walk through the valley of the shadow, for God has so ordained. But He has ordained that she shall walk in that integrity of race that was created in His wisdom and has been perpetuated in His strength. Standing in the presence of this multitude, sobered with the responsibility of the message I deliver to the young men of the South, I declare that the truth above all others to be worn unsullied and sacred in your hearts, to be surrendered to no force, sold for no price, compromised in no necessity, but cherished and defended as the covenant of your prosperity, and the pledge of peace to your children, is that the white race must dominate forever in the South, because it is the white race, and superior to that race by which its supremacy is threatened.

It is a race issue. Let us come to this point, and stand here. Here the air is pure and the light is clear, and here honor and peace abide. Juggling and evasion deceives not a man. Compromise and subservience has carried not a point. There is not a white man North or South who does not feel it stir in the gray matter of his brain and throb in his heart. Not a negro who does not feel its power. It is not a sectional issue. It speaks in Ohio and in Georgia. It speaks wherever the Anglo-Saxon touches an alien race. It has just spoken in universally approved legislation in excluding the Chinaman from our gates, not for his ignorance, vice or corruption, but because he sought to establish an inferior race in a republic fashioned in the wisdom and defended by the blood of a homogeneous people.

The Anglo-Saxon blood has dominated always and everywhere. It fed Alfred when he wrote the charter of English liberty; it gathered about Hampden as he stood beneath the oak; it thundered in Cromwell's veins as he fought his king; it humbled Napoleon at Waterloo; it has touched the desert and jungle with undying glory; it carried the drum-beat of England around the world and spread on every continent the gospel of liberty and of God; it established this republic, carved it from the wilderness, conquered it from the Indians, wrested it from England, and at last, stilling its own tumult, consecrated it forever as the home of the Anglo-Saxon, and the theater of his transcending achievement. Never one foot of it can be surrendered while that blood lives in American veins, and feeds American hearts, to the domination of an alien and inferior race.

And yet that is just what is proposed. Not in twenty years have we seen a day so pregnant with fate to this section as the sixth of next November. If President Cleveland is then defeated, which God forbid, I believe these States will be led through sorrows compared to which the woes of reconstruction will be as the fading dews of morning to the roaring flood. To dominate these States through the colored vote, with such aid as Federal patronage may debauch or Federal power determine, and thus through its chosen instruments perpetuate its rule, is in my opinion the settled purpose of the Republican party. I am appalled when I measure the passion in which this negro problem is judged by the leaders of the party. Fifteen years ago Vice-President Wilson said —and I honor his memory as that of a courageous man: "We shall not have finished with the South until we force its people to change their thought, and think as we think." I repeat these words, for I heard them when a boy, and they fell on my ears as the knell of my people's rights—"to change their thought, and make them think as we think." Not enough to have conquered our armies—to have decimated our ranks, to have desolated our fields and reduced us to poverty, to have struck the ballot from our hands and enfranchised our slaves—to have held us prostrate under bayonets while the insolent mocked and thieves plundered—but their very souls must be rifled of their faiths, their sacred traditions cudgeled from memory, and their immortal minds beaten into subjection until thought had lost its integrity, and we were forced "to think as they think." And just now General Sherman has said, and I honor him as a soldier:

"The negro must be allowed to vote, and his vote must be counted; otherwise, so sure as there is a God in heaven, you will have another war, more cruel than the last, when the torch and dagger will take the place of the muskets of well-ordered battalions. Should the negro strike that blow, in seeming justice, there will be millions to assist them."

And this general took Johnson's sword in surrender! He looked upon the thin and ragged battalions in gray, that for four years had held his teeming and heroic legions at bay. Facing them, he read their courage in their depleted ranks, and gave them a soldier's parole. When he found it in his heart to taunt these heroes with this threat, why—careless as he was twenty years ago with fire, he is even more careless now with his words. If we could hope that this problem would be settled within our lives I would appeal from neither madness nor unmanliness. But when I know that, strive as I may, I must at last render this awful heritage into the untried hands of my son, already dearer to me than my life, and that he must in turn bequeath it unsolved to his children, I cry out against the inhumanity that deepens its difficulties with this incendiary threat, and beclouds its real issue with inflaming passion.

This problem is not only enduring, but it is widening. The exclusion of the Chinese is the first step in the revolution that shall save liberty and law and religion to this land, and in peace and order, not enforced on the gallows, or at the bayonet's end, but proceeding from the heart of an harmonious people, shall secure in the enjoyment of the rights, and the control of this republic, the homogeneous people that established and has maintained it. The next step will be taken when some brave statesman, looking Demagogy in the face, shall move to call to the stranger at our gates, "Who comes there?" admitting every man who seeks a home, or honors our institutions, and whose habit and blood will run with the native current; but excluding all who seek to plant anarchy or to establish alien men or measures on our soil; and will then demand that the standard of our citizenship be lifted and the right of acquiring our suffrage be abridged. When that day comes, and God speed its coming, the position of the South will be fully understood, and everywhere approved. Until then, let us—giving the negro every right, civil and political, measured in that fullness the strong should always accord the weak—holdng him in closer friendship and sympathy than he is held by those who would crucify us for his sake—realizing that on his prosperity ours depends—let us resolve that never by external pressure, or internal division, shall he establish domination, directly or indirectly, over that race that everywhere has maintained its supremacy. Let this resolution be cast on the lines of equity and justice. Let it be the pledge of honest, safe and impartial administration, and we shall command the support of the colored race itself, more dependent than any other on the bounty and protection of government. Let us be wise and patient, and we shall secure through its acquiescence what otherwise we should win through conflict, and hold in insecurity.

All this is no unkindness to the negro—but rather that he may be led in equal rights and in peace to his uttermost good. Not in sectionalism—for my heart beats true to the Union, to the glory of which your life and heart is pledged. Not in disregard of the world's opinion—for to render back this problem in the world's approval is the sum of my ambition, and the height of human achievement. Not in reactionary spirit—but rather to make clear that new and grander way up which the South is marching to higher destiny, and on which I would not halt her for all the spoils that have been gathered unto parties since Catiline conspired, and Caesar fought. Not in passion, my countrymen, but in reason—not in narrowness, but in breadth—that we may solve this problem in calmness and in truth, and lifting its shadows let perpetual sunshine pour down on two races, walking together in peace and contentment. Then shall this problem have proved our blessing, and the race that threatened our ruin work our salvation as it fills our fields with the best peasantry the world has ever seen. Then the South—putting behind her all the achievements of her past—and in war and in peace they beggar eulogy—may stand upright among the nations and challenge the judgment of man and the approval of God, in having worked out in their sympathy, and in His guidance, this last and surpassing miracle of human government.

AGED EX-SLAVES GATHER AT HOME OF OLD MASTER.

By ROBERT TIMMONS.

Palmetto, Ga., September 26.—(Special.)—In sharp contrast to the bloody scene which was enacted in this town in April, 1899, when the riot occurred in which three negroes were shot down by a mob after they had been placed under arrest for attempting to burn the town, was the peaceful and altogether unique scene which was witnessed at the old Menefee homestead when fifteen negroes, all ex-slaves, gathered in a reunion at the home of their former master here to-day.

Never before in the history of Georgia, and probably never before in the history of the South, was there just such a gathering as that at this old Southern plantation.

The idea of holding this reunion at the home of their former master, who has been dead for a number of years, was conceived by one of the negroes present, and when it was suggested to the other ex-slaves it was received with their heartiest approval. Only one of the negroes who was present at the reunion is a resident of Palmetto, all the others coming from a distance and from different points in the State. The oldest member of the party, "Uncle" Edmund Menefee, who is 80 years old, came from near Hiram, Ga., in Cobb county, and walked the entire distance, about fifty miles, in order that he might see once more the old homestead and the other slaves with whom he was associated when a young man.

Several of the negroes who attended the reunion are residents of Atlanta and came down on the morning train, returning to the city in the evening.

The negroes who were present and who came from different parts of the State to attend the reunion were "Uncle" Edmund Menefee, of Cobb county; "Uncle" Lev Menefee, of 19 Wilson street, Atlanta; Willis Menefee Randall, of 156 Magnolia street, Atlanta; Fielding Menefee, of Cobb county; Wilson Menefee and Stewart Menefee, of Atlanta; Clarke Menefee and Taylor Slaughter, of Campbell county; Easter Menefee, Amanda Menefee and Gabriel Menefee, of Cobb county, and his mother, "Aunt" Hennie Menefee, the old family cook, who estimates her age at 90 years; Jennie Menefee, John Menefee and Harvie Menefee.

These are the only living ex-slaves of about 125 who belonged to the estate of Major Menefee, and who were given their freedom by him after the war had closed. As was customary after being given their freedom, the negroes took the name of their former master.

Each of these negroes is well-to-do, many of them are property owners. Most of them followed the business which was taught them as slaves, that of tilling the soil. They say they are in the South to stay. It was estimated that the value of the property owned by them is about $10,000.

The white persons who were present and witnessed the celebration of these ex-slaves were: Mrs. M. A. Wiley, of Palmetto; Mrs. S. M. Dean, of Atlanta; Mrs. John H. Covin, of Hogansville, all daughters of Major Willis Menefee; Dr. W. S. Zellars, one of the oldest inhabitants of Palmetto, who was the physician employed by Major Menefee to attend the slaves before the war; Mrs. Maggie Dean Morris, of Atlanta; Willis Menefee Timmons, of Atlanta; Mrs. E. K. Farmer, of Fitzgerald, Ga.; Miss Stevie Timmons, of Atlanta; Mrs. Howard Wooding, of Hogansville; B. E. L. Timmons, Jr., of Inman; Thomas Covin, of Hogansville, and B. H. Timmons, of Atlanta, all grandchildren of Major Menefee, and Miss Mabel Brown and Mrs. T. P. Zellars, together with several other friends of the family.

The old Menefee home is located about half a mile from the center of town, and is a typical ante-bellum residence. It is situated some distance back from the road and is reached by a broad gravel walk leading up to the large stone steps between an avenue of cedar trees. As it was before the war the large yard immediately in front of the house is filled with all kinds of beautiful and sweet smelling flowers, vines and shrubbery indigenous to Southern soil, among which the humming birds flit on their honey-gathering expeditions all during the summer days.

In front of the house, across the Atlantic & West Point railroad, and to the rear, after passing a pine and oak grove, stretch acres and acres of rich corn and cotton fields which compose the plantation. The home and plantation is now owned by Mrs. M. A. Wiley, the oldest living daughter of Major Menefee.

When the old ex-slaves began to arrive in the morning it was an interesting sight to a member of a younger generation of whites to watch them as they wandered about over the place, viewing the scenes so familiar to them in the days before the war when they were a part of the property which made up this Southern plantation. Many of them had never visited the plantation since several years after the war, when they left to provide for themselves.

The intensely religious nature, so characteristic of

the negro, was clearly shown as they walked about the yard and through the house with uncovered heads to show their reverence for the place where they had spent what each said was the happiest period of their lives. A touching scene was witnessed when they were carried into the spacious parlor of the home and shown the portrait of their former master. They stood with bowed heads, many of them weeping, and each speaking with praise unrestrained of the master who had treated them so kindly when they were slaves.

They visited the dairy, the stables, the apple orchard and the hill in the rear of the "big" house, where was situated the "quarters" during the time they lived on the plantation as slaves. Many interesting incidents of the former days were remembered and recited in their quaint negro dialect by the older members of the party.

At the noon hour, as was her custom before the war, old "Aunt" Hennie, the cook, blew the conch shell which had so often called them to their meals, and they gathered under the wide-spreading oaks in the rear of the house, where a table loaded down with good things to eat had been prepared for them.

After the meal was finished the children and grandchildren of their former master gathered in the yard under the tree and listened to the negroes as they related incidents of the days of slavery before and during the war.

They never tired of singing the praise of their master, "Marse Willis," and their mistress, "Miss Jannette." They told of how well they had been treated as slaves and of how, though they wanted freedom, yet when freedom came they wanted to remain on the same plantation and continue to work for their mistress, after the death of their master. They told of

" Uncle Gabriel,"
52 years old.

" Aunt " Hennie,
90 years old.

" Uncle " Lev,
77 years old.

" Uncle " Fielding,
50 years old.

" Uncle " Willis,
63 years old.

" Uncle " Edmond,
80 years old.

Former slaves of Major Willis Menefee, who attended remarkable reunion held at old Menefee Homestead in Palmetto.

how their master had taught them to be religious, to be neat and clean, to be always honest and give the proper respect to the whites. These lessons, they said, had remained with them and they were teaching them to their children.

"Uncle" Edmund, the oldest member of the party, and the one who had walked fifty miles to attend the reunion, told of how he had remained with his mistress during the war and had gladly protected her, the children and the house while Sherman and his yankees were marching through Palmetto.

Many old plantation melodies were sung and each one of the fifteen present joined in. The music was of that quaint, perfectly harmonious kind such as only negroes can make.

The songs and stories continued till late in the afternoon, and before the gathering broke up it was agreed that each year the reunion would be held on the old plantation.

RACES IN HARMONY; SOUTH SAFE AS HOME.

COULD NOT DEPORT NEGRO IF SUCH WAS DESIRED—THE RACES ARE MORE IN HARMONY THAN THEY HAVE BEEN AT ANY TIME SINCE THE CIVIL WAR.

EX-GOVERNOR W. J. NORTHEN, OF GEORGIA.

In connection with the wide discussion concerning the subject of lynching, violence and mob law that has followed the publication of the communication of Bishop Candler on the matter in the Constitution, the following interview with former Governor W. J. Northen is sure to prove both interesting and profitable.

It will be remembered in this connection that Mr. Northen has not only been a close and careful student of the entire subject, but was pertinently, if not personally, responsible for the introduction of the anti-lynching legislation during his term of office which still presents the legal side of the matter in the State statutes of Georgia.

Former Governor Northen also furnishes in the interview certain statistics and chapters of history regarding the anti-lynching movement that are absolutely essential in the discussion of the subject. Perhaps the greatest and most prominent feature brought out by this student is his cheerful, optimistic view of the situation and facts which prove that Georgia, at least, has traveled far on the road of solving this much mooted question.

Where some men have painted the South as a dangerous and unsafe place to live in, he points with facts rather than arguments to prove that home, sweet home, is never sweeter and safer than right among the green fields of Georgia. Where some point to the exile or ostracism of the negro as the only solution, ex-Governor Northen shows that the problem is already well advanced toward a peaceful and satisfactory settlement in a better understanding between the two races.

While he opposes lynching and mob violence from any standpoint, he seems to almost deplore the fact that there is not some greater punishment for the crime of rape than the sentence of death, which the law provides. He criticises, too, the unscrupulous press in painting a reign of lawlessness and carnage regardless of facts that furnishes erroneous impressions that are quickly grasped by the newspapers of the North and reprinted to show that the South is still grappling with a problem that makes a visit to Dixie land a trip attended with jeopardy while the erection of a home in the Southland demands little less than military protection.

When approacheed on the subject, ex-Governor Northen said that he had kept up with the discussions of the matter as they have appeared in the newspapers. He was strongly of the opinion that no considerable portion of the people of the South were in favor of mob violence or lynch law, while so far as Georgia is concerned, he said that he could state authoritatively that the sentiment was in favor of allowing the law to take its course in the settlement of justice.

"If you will pardon the personal reference, let me say, during my administration I had occasion to make a very thorough official investigation, that fully satisfied me that the people of this State, as a body, were in the fullest sympathy with the administration of the law and that they were ready to uphold it at any and all hazard, whatever the nature of the crime demanding punishment."

In further proof of his confidence in the people he said:

"When I left the capitol I left on file a mass of correspondence covering, to my satisfaction, the position of the people of this State on mob violence and lynching. Taking as the starting point, I filed the admirable essay by the then distinguished Chief Justice of the Supreme Court, as read before the State Bar Association, pleading for the maintenance of the law and the authority of the courts in the prosecution of criminals and the punishments for crime, whatever the violation and however damnable the outrage. The courts, he proclaimed, are sufficient and he inveighed strongly against the fury and the wreck of a maddened mob.

"Apprehending that I might have occasion to enforce the observance of the law in the suppression of a mob, I addressed letters to the daily newspapers in the State to know whether I would be supported in the policy. From every daily paper I received not only favorable replies, but in each case the statements were very strongly put.

"I then addressed letters to each one of the superior court judges and the solicitors general of the several courts, to know whether or not they were in sympathy with the sentiments of the distinguished Chief Justice as expressed in the essay to which I have alluded. To a man I found them to be just as strong.

"Following the matter further, I wrote to the sheriffs over the State and I found them ready to support the law to the fullest extent of their authority.

"All this correspondence I left on file at the capitol,

attesting the loyalty of the officers of the State to the majesty of the law.

"When the General Assembly met I had a conference with prominent members of the judiciary committee as to the sufficiency of law for the punishment of mob violence and kindred lawlessness, and it was agreed that absolute security would be effected by some additional legislation. Hon. Warner Hill, chairman of this committee, was selected to frame such statute, and it passed both houses without a dissenting vote. This statute authorizes the sheriff or other officer in charge to suppress mob violence by arresting the parties so engaged and placing them in the common jail to be dealt with as the law directs; it declares that any citizen engaged in mobbing or lynching is guilty of felony and on conviction to be punished by imprisonment in the penitentiary; and should death result from such mob violence the person causing said death shall be subject to indictment and trial for murder. The statute further provides that the sheriff shall be punished for failure to do his duty. The law gives the sheriff authority to summon to his aid, with arms, any number of citizens he may need to suppress the mob, and to take human life, if it be necessary, to enforce the law.

"When this bill became law I sent a copy to each sheriff in the State, accompanied by the following letter:

"'State of Georgia, Executive Department, Atlanta, Ga., December 19, 1893.—My Dear Sir: I enclose you herewith copy of bill introduced by Hon. Warner Hill, passed unanimously by the recent General Assembly, and approved this day.

"'I send you the bill thus early that you may at once know its provisions and that I may apprise you of the authority given you in the Act, as well as the responsibility now put upon you to preserve the peace and honor of the State.

" 'The General Assembly, by unanimous action, has pronounced death by mob violence murder, and declared that all citizens who become parties thereto are subject to indictment and trial under such charge. You will observe, further, that the Act not only authorizes you to summon to your aid any and all the citizens of your county, in your efforts to suppress mob violence and lawlessness, but it very properly pronounces failure to respond on the part of such citizens so summoned a misdemeanor, and upon conviction they will be duly punished under the law.

" 'I can hardly believe that any officer of the law in this State will so far fail in duty as to deserve the punishment prescribed in section 2 of this Act, yet I am candid to say that I suggested and I am, therefore, responsible for this enactment, as I desired to make it absolutely certain that another case of mob violence should never be possible in this State.

" 'The Act, therefore, compels both the citizen and the officer to discharge their duties under penalty of the law.

" 'The honor of the State, as far as your jurisdiction extends, is now in your hands, and I shall watch with great interest the outcome of this new legislation.

" 'Your strong letter, received some months ago, assuring me of your determined purpose to aid in suppressing lawlessness, has had much to do with the passage of this bill, and I am constrained to believe you will do your whole duty and that mob law in Georgia is now at an end.

" 'W. J. NORTHEN, Governor.'

"I have given you these facts to demonstrate three things:

"1. That every court officer is fully ready to do his full duty in the enforcement of the law.

"2. That the machinery of the courts is sufficient to punish adequately and fully, as provided by law, every crime possible to human villainy.

"3. That the sentiment of the people in this State is strongly against mob violence, especially as expressed in lynching. If this were not true, the newspapers in the State would not have given to me the expressions stated to you a moment ago. If it were not true, the bill that became law would not have passed the General Assembly of the State without a dissenting vote. The lawmakers represented the people, and they put the views of the people into State enactment. The sentiment of the people of this State is unquestionably against mob violence and lynching."

In answer to the question as to whether or not there had been lynchings since the enactment of that law, he replied:

"Yes, and there have been in this State and every other State violations of every criminal law in the Code, but that does not indicate that the people are not pronounced against such iniquities. The question to which I am making reply is: Does any considerable portion of the people at the South favor mob violence or lynch law?"

When asked to suggest some remedy, the ex-Governor continued:

"I believe the people in the rural districts are as much entitled to police protection as the people in the cities. I do not make the suggestion because of the presence of the negroes any more than I would make the suggestion to the cities because of their absence, but on general conditions that demand protection. Every county in this State and in every other State, North or South, should have a police force efficient and active. The sheriff should be chief of such county police, and see that they are vigilant. This will not only largely eliminate the little remaining spirit there is still among our people to deal summary vengeance upon outlaws, but it would furnish such protection as to prevent crimes of all kinds in the rural sections. It is well to say, as you have, doubtless, oberved, that there has been not only less occasion for mob violence because of assaults, but that the people have more generally refrained from violence and awaited action by the courts. The relations between the races are not so antagonistic as formerly, but far more cooperative. To believe this, you have only to recall the conditions that existed soon after the war when the ku-klux were believed to be necessary to the safety of the people. After these, came the vigilance committees, and now, if we had the county police, regulated by law, the situation would be largely, if not completely, met.

"Next, I would be glad to see the sheriffs devote one entire session of their State convention to the discussion of matters pertaining to their duties in subduing mobs and enforcing the law. Such discussion will not only bring helpful suggestions to officers of the law, but it will tend to create most healthful public opinion and establish authority.

"The great objection, as stated oftentimes, is the necessity for the presence of the outraged victim before the court during the trial of the alleged outlaw. To remedy this, I call your attention to a provision of the Code of 1882, section 4663, as follows:

"'It shall be the duty of the judges of the superior courts to make a special report annually to the Governor of this State previous to the meeting of the General Assembly, and by him to be submitted to the Legislature, of all such defects, omissions or imperfections in this Code, as experience on their several circuits may suggest.' Surely, the judiciary of the State can suggest some enactment that will meet the demands of the case and prevent the humiliation complained of in case of court trial.

"After having expressed myself thus far at your request, may I now be allowed to say there has been a good deal of morbid and extravagant statements about conditions at the South upon the subject of outrages and lynchings. There is not a better civilization in any State or section in this Union than in Georgia, and at the South. I have lived here all my life, and I have been all over the United States, and I have yet to find a place for which I would exchange a home in Georgia or at the South. I have lived among negroes all my life, and, like the distinguished bishop, I do not want to live where there are none. I will trust them in every relation far more confidently than I would the mongrel population of self-announced socialists, anarchists and outlaws, who do the menial service of other sections. We do not want to deport the negroes. We could not if we so desired. How can you force 10,000,000 of people to leave the country, when they exercise the same civil rights as are accorded to you? If they consented to go, where is the country accessible in which they would be more acceptable than to you? Who would receive them, if you cast them off? They now have to their credit upon the tax books more than a half billion dollars worth of property. Who would buy at the prices they would, later, demand for their holdings? If these conditions were all met, the expense of transportation would burden the government beyond recovery in its most prosperous days. Who would buy for them their furnishings and the lands upon which they must settle?

"The negro furnishes almost exclusively the farm labor at the South. If all other possible conditions could be met satisfactorily their leaving in a body or gradually would paralyze the agricultural conditions at the South beyond recovery for three generations. Let it be understood that the negroes are here to stay, and we are going to see that they behave themselves or punish them with the extreme penalty of the law when they deserve and give them fullest credit when their conduct so demands.

"The better classes of the negroes have shown themselves quite as much in favor of the death penalty for the outlaws of their race who commit assaults as are the white people themselves. There is no longer that disposition to conceal and protect these criminals against full and proper punishment. When this punishment is administered uniformly by due process of law and not by the barbarous burnings by the mob, you will find the most active co-operation on their part in bringing the criminal to the tribunal designated to punish crime.

"For all these years I have had occasion to watch closely the relations between the races in this State, and I say to you, most positively, there has not been a time since the war when we were more in harmony than we are to-day.

"Have you not observed that a great deal of misinformation is given to the press and scattered over the country to the great damage of our honor as a State and our best material interests? A case in point occurred only a short time since when we were told that a white man and a negro had committed an outrage on an old white woman in one of our lower counties and that both these outlaws had been promptly lynched. The next day we were told the outrages had not been committed, and, of course, the lynching had not taken place. Again, we constantly see something like this: 'A villanious negro committed a fearful crime in this community yesterday and he is being pursued by an infuriated crowd of men. He will be lynched as soon as captured.' Why not wait until the lynching occurs? There seems to be a morbid appetite on the part of some correspondents and some newspapers that are afraid of being 'scooped' and it is gratified to the great damage of our civilization and the honor of the State.

"There is no crime known to me more villainous and damning than the one unnamed. If there were punishment greater than death I would be glad to see it administered to the guilty outlaw, under due process of law before the courts, but I protest now, as I have for all these years, against mob law and lynching. Our law properly pronounces such brutality murder, and no crime, however heinous, can justify it. I have shown you that our people do not countenance it, and any statement to the contrary is untrue. We are now putting all the idle negroes to work and the better negroes are helping to this end. Vice and crime have greatly decreased among them and we are practically free from trouble. Let us stop the continued abuse of the negro and rather help him to be useful to himself and the community. Commend him freely and generously and publicly, if you will, when he does well, and punish him severely in the courts when he is vicious, and let that be the end of it. We have no occasion for a constant crying out. We have peace and abundant prosperity. Just let us say so, publish the crimes of the people if it is best, but let us be sure they have been committed before we say so."

MUST PUT DOWN THE MOB OR BE PUT DOWN BY IT.

By BISHOP WARREN A. CANDLER, D.D.,
Of the Methodist Church.

The lynching mania can no longer be considered a local, or sectional evil. It has spread to every part of our country and shows itself as the manifestation of a spirit that deserves the reprobation of the good everywhere without regard to party or place.

It is something worse than unfair for the people of the North to treat the subject as if it were a peculiar sin of the South, and it is something worse than a mistake for the people of the South to defend it as if it were their especial besetment about which they felt a self-convicting sensitiveness. It is the duty of all good people in every part of our country to unite in putting down the mob. For let us be well assured that the good people will put down the mob, or the mob will put down the good people.

When a lynching occurs, the law is more truly lynched than is the victim of the mob's fury. It is an outburst of anarchy, and not an eruption of righteous indignation against an atrocious crime.

In defense of lynching, it is sometimes said: "Stop the outrages that provoke lynching and the lynching will cease." But pray tell which outrage is meant? If reference to the horrible crime of rape is intended, it is enough to say in reply that it is not the cause of one-fourth the lynchings which occur in the United States. Two years since, for example, the figures for a year showed only sixteen cases of ravishing against 128 lynchings. In the case at Evansville, Ind., the original sin which gave rise to the lynching was the shooting of a policeman. But the mob sent a load of buckshot into the breast of a young girl of 15 years of age, who was in no wise involved. How can such reckless fury ever cure crime, or arrest disorder? Is there one home more secure or one life more safe by reason of such horrible outbursts?

Who composed this Indiana mob? Were its leaders men who were incontrollably jealous for morality and justice? On the contrary, the arrests made subsequent to the lynching showed among the leaders three professional gamblers, three men known to the police as desperate characters, and one man who had been guilty of killing another some years ago. Is it not clear that this lynching was fomented and carried out by a lot of blood-thirsty scapegraces, who had not the slightest interest in anything good? They are the sort who find pleasure in the bloody brutalities of the prize fight. And yet men of respectability were found foolish enough to apologize for the atrocities.

And such are the men, generally, who organize mob violence. How delighted they must be when decent people rush into print to defend, if not to eulogize, their diabolical deeds! Is it not time decent people put their pens to better use? The mob which they eulogize to-day will turn upon its defenders to-morrow. The taste for blood grows with indulgence.

Lynch law, I repeat, is anarchy, and anarchy is always the forerunner of destruction in republics. This evil strikes at the very heart of our civil institutions. If unchecked it will increase, and eventually become unendurable by the vicious even. Men will grow so weary of it that they will welcome any sort of strong hand which will undertake to put it down, even the hand of tyranny. They will argue that the tyranny of one strong, wise man is preferable to the many-headed tyranny of a brainless mob, as, indeed, it is. Then the hour for the "man on horseback" will have struck and he will appear. The anarchy of Sulla and Marius produced Caesarism, with all the dreadful consequences it drew after it. The spirit of mobocracy in the Grecian republics made Philip of Macedon possible and opened the way for Alexander. Robespierre and his rioters gave Napoleon his chance. They slew the liberty which they professed to love.

And let no man suppose that such an outcome is impossible in our land and time. The American people are as quick as any to adore a military hero, and they can make one out of as small amount of the raw material as any nation that ever kissed a sword or bowed to a plume. Witness the election of Jackson and the "rough rider" to the highest office. Moreover, it should be remembered that we turn out of the military academy of the nation annually more than a hundred young men whose future turns on the use of the sword. They are generally men of worldly honor and ambition. Many of them come from influential families, and have the influence of such connections back of them. Would it be a strange thing if in all their number there should be found one capable of seizing power in the name of order? Or, would it be a matter of wonder if the people, having grown weary of disorder, should gladly welcome a strong, educated man of honor, who should appear and promise them peace and security? Stranger things have happened.

Depend upon it, no nation ever retains liberty after it ceases to maintain law. Lynch law protects no home, but does rather pull down the strongest defense of all the homes in the commonwealth. Our homes are sheltered by law, and they are not shielded by lawlessness.

We have problems enough to solve in this country, to be sure. But we have no problem which cannot be solved by the practice of personal and civic righteousness every day. The man who will not try that remedy has no right to propose any other. In the end, all other solutions will be found worse than vain.

With reference to the various picturesque proposals which are periodically made to cure all our ills, it is, perhaps, not unkind to say that the silence of their authors would be more valuable than their speech. It seems that there is a certain amount of periodical space to be filled and a certain number of men who live by filling it with their pieces. When the weather gets warm and they find it hard to write anything that will be read what else can these men do but fall to solving all the problems of the nation—the South in particular—in order to settle their own pressing question, "How shall I manage to say something that will sell and provide for my board bill?" And then, too, the "chautauqua season" is a very dangerous period of the year, especially during those years when the Congress of the United States is not in session and the thrifty statesman who is deficient in a sense of responsibility for his words, is "out for the stuff," and when platform managers, who have an eye for gate receipts only, are out hunting for "drawing" sensationalists, without regard for the kind of things that the sensation-mongers may pour out of their easy-acting mouths.

What a pity these men undertake to handle matters so serious and so complex! Yea, what a peril! Adventurous sportsmen discharging firearms in a powder-house would not be a greater menace to good order and security.

Good men, helped of God, can solve all our questions if they can only find a way to muzzle the agitators, or if they can find a way to switch the agitators off on subjects that they can talk about without endangering the peace of society. I think, for example, that the race question could be settled if we can find out how to silence men who make merchandise out of its discussion. For one, I am not nearly so afraid of the race question as I am of the race of "chautauqua platformers and performers!" The apprehension of the mischief they may do to all the races in our country haunts me all through the dog-days. I know how to get on with the negroes, for I was brought up with them. But one of these problem-solving talkers scares me. I am not afraid of him for what he really is, but for what some well-meaning people may take him to be. A bleating calf jumping suddenly from under a chinquapin bush may make a really gentle horse run away; or a moon-eyed horse hitched alongside a reliable nag may shy at what he thinks is a bogie and frighten his mate into the most dangerous misbehavior. It is thus some good men have been led to apologize for lynching. They have seen nightmares until they are prepared to conjure with a real horror in order to down a ghost.

The situation in the South is one of difficulty, of course. So is the situation in Chicago, or that of Paris, or that of London, or that of New York. Our homes in the South are safer than the homes of Chicago. Give me the negro any time, in preference to the anarchists and free lovers. In fact, I do not wish to live in any country where there are no negroes.

But if our difficulties were a thousand-fold greater than they are, lynchings would not remove them. Such deeds of lawlessness multiply all our troubles. If these things must be anywhere in our country, let them be confined to the North, where a denser population, composed of all sorts of heterogeneous elements, furnish greater provocations to them, and, perforce, more excuse for them.

We do not want any such barbarities to defend our Southern civilization.

RACES MUST SEPARATE, ASSERTS BISHOP TURNER.

One of the features of the mass meeting yesterday afternoon at the People's tabernacle was the address of Bishop Henry M. Turner on the subject, "Is the Pulpit Equal to the Times? If so, Why this Quibble that Frightens the Common People and Seemingly Paralyzes Labor in the Farming Sections?"

Bishop Turner devoted a considerable portion of his time in replying to Dr. H. S. Bradley, who in an address last Monday declared that the separation of the races was a chimerical proposition. Bishop Turner declared that separation of the races was the only solution of the race problem, though he did not expect all the negroes to rush out of the country. What he wishes is for the negro to be given an opportunity to go to Africa if he so desires.

He spoke as follows:

"Mr. Chairman—Among the remarks that I shall make on this occasion will be a few in reply to Rev. Dr. H. S. Bradley, who fills one of the first pulpits of Atlanta, and is the pastor of a congregation cultured and refined.

"I venerate the distinguished divine, Rev. Dr. H. S. Bradley, scholarly, eloquent, humane, as he is, and I believe he is a Christian gem of the first water. Indeed, I have received a personal recognition from him that I have been accorded by no other white minister in the city of Atlanta, while all have treated me with respect. But it so happens that God made me out of that kind of material which enables me to rise above personal considerations sufficiently to agree with my enemies and differ with my friends when the question at issue requires it. Personal likes and dislikes have nothing to do with my honest opinions.

"The learned doctor last Monday night, the 21st instant, delivered an elegant and rhetorical speech before a mass meeting of my race (and I was present) against the separation of the races—I mean the white and black races, or, as the Africans say, the Buchra man and the Otutu man. He hurled his florid remarks against negro emigration, segregation, any form of separation or any movement that would contemplate negro concretion, civilly or politically, and as I saw it presented one of the most eloquent and illogical addresses I have heard for a great while—not because he is wanting in logical ability and attainments, for I have heard him both in the pulpit, on the platform, and have read after him, but because he was handling a subject which he had never studied with a view of its practical results, as the early history of Rome, of North America, of South America and of Australia, and indeed the history of all peoples and nations would have shown the folly of his position. For emigration is the philosophy of ancient and modern history.

"The bulk of white men know but little about the inner feelings and idiosyncrasies of the negro, and when they speak about black men emigrating to better their conditions they signally fail by reason of the fact that it is not a question that concerns them enough to give it deep and protracted thought. I know there are many white men who ride into popularity by pretending to know all about the negro, but they only know the ignorant and scullion side of him.

"In this country, where white represents God, and black the devil, but little thought is given to the black man's future. Everything that concerns the negro is whittled down to the present contingencies, and the eternal .future which involves and comprehends change, revolution, mutation and the mighty destiny of races, is but little thought of, and if the negro does not think about it himself, it will receive but little attention and our status as a race, to use the language of the elder Judge Lumpkin, is so ignoble, and the foolish scarecrow of social equality has become such a hobgoblin with the ignorant masses, that we are further apart in spirit and sympathy than heaven and hell. We are as ignorant of each other as races as if we did not live in the same world. The very conditions that surround and confront us forbid a white man from having any real knowledge of the negro, and I could bring a hundred illustrations to establish this fact. It was verified the other night in Dr. Bradley's address when he said the negroes were American citizens, and do not wish to be segregated. I grant that the doctor represented a large portion, for as the Savannah News says, 'The negro is not yet a nation building race,' but if he will put a steamer between here and Africa and make the rates of travel as cheap as white emigrants get from Europe to America 4,000,000 will leave as soon as they can adjust their little affairs. While I am not burdened to death with intelligence, I have too much sense to say that all would go. I do not know as half would go. Jahn in his Biblical archaeology says that not half of the children of Israel ever left Egypt for the promised land, but the vast multitude which remained has never been heard of from that day till this. No people in the world's history, who were not self-reliant and who are not prompted by their inner nature to sue for better conditions, have ever reached the plane of respectability. Indeed, they are invariably crushed out of existence and exterminated. I have been reading history fifty years and over and if there is any exception to this rule, outside possibly of the Saxons who were absorbed, and also did much of the absorbing by virtue of being of the same color and having the most beautiful women on earth at that time, I would be pleased to have them pointed out.

"The doctor says the negro is an American citizen. I wish he was correct. Twelve millions of colored people of the United States would throw their hats, parasols and umbrellas heaven high, if possible, if his declaration about the citizenship of the negro was a reality, or could be established. Surely the doctor has not been apprised of the fact that the conclave in Washington, D. C., called the United States Supreme Court, has issued a legislative decision taking away every vestige of his civil rights, and in the recent Alabama case has declared his political rights a nullity, and outside of the right to pay taxes and work on the roads he has not a single right that would prompt him to be a man. I would mention the degradation this decision, or these decisions (for there are three of them), have inflicted upon the negro, in detail, but it would be too voluminous and do no good; but I will give $500 if any man will show me such a decision from any court of last resort in the history of the world. Its uniqueness stands in the fact that they legislated and decided at the same time. No instance of the kind is found in the chronicles of the nation.

"But just at this point I beg to ask the doctor if he could have any respect for a man, or any set of men, who would sit quietly under the condition of things that confront the negro in this country? If he wants to know what I mean, just let him color his face (for white is not a color) and attempt to be a man and a gentleman for one day, and he will understand the meaning thoroughly. We are daily the subjects of comment and misrepresentation. God is charged with folly for attempting to make a man and failing to complete His job, and he is assigned to the realm of inferiority, and yet more laws have been enacted by the different legislatures of the country, and more judicial decisions have been delivered and proclaimed against this piece of inferiority called negro than have been issued against any people since time began. It would appear that the negro is the greatest man on earth if we are to judge from the judicial decisions in the code books of the country to keep him down.

"The Pilgrim fathers did not have to contend with one-half of the legal fetters, but they left the old country and sought a land where they could develop the mighty forces that heaven had implanted in their natures, and the result is a great and powerful people have been developed. Which does the doctor have the highest respect for—the early settlers of Plymouth in Massachusetts and Jamestown, Va., or the docile negro who will not try to help himself?

"I have been singled out in this country as the chief factor in the African emigration movement, and as such I believe that I have received all of a hundred thousand letters, some of them containing dozens and dozens of names, who are clamoring for transportation conveniences and cheap rates from this to the land of our ancestors, so they can return to Africa without having to pay their way to New York City, then to Liverpool, England, and then to Africa, which they have to do at present, costing them more on the cars to New York than white people have to pay from Queenstown, Liverpool, Hamburg and other points to come to New York, Philadelphia, Boston, New Orleans and Savannah.

"Think of it, 557 steamers, besides sailing ships, are hugging the shores of Africa the year round from Europe, and not one from the United States. These European steamers, carrying to her ports hundreds of millions, if not a billion dollars of commerce annually, and not the worth of a nickel of commerce from the United States. Some of us have been trying for years to get this government to subsidize a ship for mail purposes, and let it serve as a transport for emigration and commerce, as a start to the movement, but up to the present our efforts have been fruitless. President Harrison would have done something, but he was afraid of public sentiment. President Cleveland saw the philosophy of it, but was contending with the Hawaiian question and disposed of it by saying time would make it all right; and time will do it. This nation, or its aggregated people, will either have to open up a highway to Africa for the discontented black man or the negro question will flinder this government.

"There will be no peace to the United States as long as the negro question is an issue. Might may hold the scepter and sway legislative and judicial power for a time, and even suppress free speech and tyrannize over the dissatisfaction of a people for a while, but right will step to the front in its own good time and twist the scepter from the hands of might, for the reason that God is right. A United States Senator from a Southern State said to me some time ago: 'I am opposed to your emigration agitation, especially about returning to Africa in any numbers. You are keeping up an unnecessary excitement,' but finally said: 'Remember, Turner, that I am opposed to it as a white man, as your race furnishes us with a cheap and obedient labor; but if I was a negro I will be d——d if I would not leave this country before the sun goes down.'

"I do not regard Hon. John Temple Graves as the quintessence of infallibility, especially when he is discussing and commenting upon the intellectual and moral status of my race, as he represented them in some respects, in Chautauqua and Chicago, while he only expressed the current opinion of the white people generally; but the remedy that he pointed out to the American people, in regard to the existing condition of things, in my opinion, and in the opinion of sober thinking people generally, raises him to a national majesty, and makes him the greatest statesman and philosopher in the land. Among the notable and illustrious men of the country Mr. Graves towers above them all. Bismarck never offered to Germany, nor Gladstone to England, a wiser measure and a more philosophical proposition, than Mr. Graves has offered to the American people. He is evidently a widely read scholar, a master logician, and has the courage of his convictions, and defies public criticism, when he tells the white and black man in this country they must separate, for separation is the ultimatum, and that alone will bring peace to this nation.

"I will tell the black man what Mr. Graves thought, but was reluctant to express. Your very existence depends upon separation. At present there is no Christian unity, much less civil and political unity. A shameful division prevails.

"When I speak of separation I do not say that everybody will go or must go. I am only contending that there should be a highway made across the Atlantic (only 3,350 miles from the city hall of New York) for such black men and women as are self-reliant and have those manhood aspirations that God planted in them and degrading laws will intensify. We are not clamoring for rich men, or men of respectable means. We want smart, energetic and self-reliant men. If Australia could be made one of the greatest countries on earth by penal convicts, who would dare say that respectable colored men could not also build up a nation?

"It was also proclaimed the other night that Liberia was a failure and had played out. I know Liberia. I know Muhlenburg Station. I presided over an annual conference there of ordained ministers, and I am prepared to say that a finer republic is not found on earth than Liberia, consisting of 35,000 civilized and a million and a half of heathen people. Monrovia, the capital, with a population of 6,000, is one of the most beautiful cities, as seen from the ocean, that either England or America can present.

"The state house, presidential mansion, cabinet departments, and a score of cities in the republic, and the ships that stand in her various harbors, tell their own story, and there is not a bar-room in the republic to curse and ultimately damn her young men. If Georgia has played out, then Liberia has played out, but I grant that Liberia needs immigrants, and a number of business men to help develop and bring into utilization her resources. I mean her gold, silver, diamonds, coal and to till the richest soil on earth.

"I must not make my remarks too long. Let me say, however, that the negro is the richest man in the world, if he had intelligence enough to know it. We will get that intelligence, however, in God's own good time. The American negro, with a few exceptions, is the lowest specimen of the African tribes. The superior African sold us inferior Africans to the white men. We were slaves hundreds and thousands of years to our African masters before we were sold to this country to become the slaves of our white masters; but this lower type has to return in numbers, to civilize and Christianize the higher type, and the white man has to help us to do it, and God will see he does it, or the nation that owes us $40,000,000,000 for two hundred years' work performed and services rendered will commence to wane and end in broken fragments, like the Roman empire. I grant that the outlook for the future between the two races looks far more pacific than what it did.

"The assistance rendered by our white friends to Morris Brown college, especially, where we hope to train African missionaries, and elevate that portion of our race, who will live and die here, seems to tinge the future with brighter prospects. But, God sent the negro here through his negative providence, to imbibe civilization and Christianity from this giant white race, and then redeem the land of his ancestors, and he must do it and will, ultimately, do it."

RACE SEGREGATION.

An Address by Bishop Lucius H. Holsey, D.D., of the C. M. E. Church, before the National Sociological Society, at the Lincoln Temple Congregational Church.

Ladies and Gentlemen, and Fellow Citizens: Perhaps there is no question or problem that confronts the wisdom, the patriotism, and philanthropy of American citizenship, greater and farther reaching in effect and results than the perplexing and momentous question of the racial problem.

According to public sentiment and private judgment, according to the construction of the fabric of society, the enactment of its laws and their execution, there is a serious racial question; a question that strikes deep into the recesses of American life, taking hold of the basis of government and its advancing and expanding civilization; a profound question, upon which hinges the peace, happiness, and prosperity of all the people, and the possibilities and destiny of a great African race.

From any view-point we may take, it is silly, if not madness, to ignore or set at naught this great problem of the races. That there is a problem, no one, who has surveyed the field and weighed and measured the active and operative factors therein contained, can deny. Seeking for the permanent adjustment of this question, and its satisfactory solution, a multiplicity of theories, of many degrees and forms, have been presented for consideration. It also appeals to the candid thought of the North and of the South, and to the patience of the black race, who, by no design of their own, are yet the cause of conflicting forces. It may be presumed as axiomatic that to every problem that arises out of the government of a nation there may be found a method of adjustment and solution. Just as sure as all the parties concerned seek the solution with patriotism and philanthropic impulse, any question thus arising may be settled in a way to preserve the peace, protect the civil order, and advance the interest of all.

As our subject is "race segregation," or the separation of the races, we shall state what is meant. Segregation does not mean colonization, exportation or emigration. It does not mean the banishment of Afro-Americans to any foreign country or realm, within the limits or beyond the limits of our flag. Neither does it mean for Afro-Americans to be sent to the Pacific islands, acquired and held by our Federal government, but it means that the government set apart some territory, or parts of some of the public domain, for the specific purpose of forming a State or States for qualified Afro-American citizens. This is what we understand and advocate as segregation, and this is what we shall proceed to elaborate and set forth as clearly and briefly as we can.

The first reason for segregation lies in the dominant fact that the infinite volume of racial prejudice makes it impossible for the two separate and distinct races to live together in the same territory in harmonious relations, each demanding equal political rights and equal citizenship. Whether prejudice is an attribute of human nature or the cultivated and cherished adjunct of circumstances is a subtle question which we do not now attempt to discuss. But we know from history and by experience that it does exist, and it is as old as those racial traits of physical character by which one race is distinguished from another. Whether fundamental or cultivated, it has played a great part in the world's civilization and the history of the nations, often affecting the interests of universal humanity. It is deepest and bitterest and has its most prolonged conflict when it hinges upon opposite racial peculiarities and characteristics. In other words, prejudice is the strongest and the most enduring where extremes in natural racial physical distinctions meet, and where it is assumed that one is inferior to the other, because of color, previous condition or of tribal or natural origin and relation. Although it is difficult to assimilate very distinct and dissimilar races and peoples, yet it is the clearest thing to impartial decision that the Afro-American people accept and absorb very readily the pith and germs of civic life or take on the present civilization. It also seems that, so far as the Southern portion of our country is concerned, this prejudice is not only destined to continue indefinitely, but is on the increase and growing in volume, force and depth. The ruling people of the South not only make it a special end to be obtained and to dominate the South with it, but efforts are made to spread it in the North and circulate it through all parts of the nation, so as to make the down-trodden African people to be despised by those who have shown their friendship for them in the past. The bitterness, the antagonisms, the racial feuds and bloody riots in which the black man is the extreme sufferer, grow out of this fearful element in human nature. As the races now stand, and as they must stand in the South, there is no power inherent in government to remove it or destroy it, or even to ameliorate or soften its force or ferocity. Those elements and factors by which the phases of social and political life have been changed and made to fit and harmonize with new relations and conditions have no perceptible effect or bearing in the present case. Time measured by decades and years, the recognized agency and the ancient power that revolutionize thought, opinions, judgment and actions, cannot change or destroy this old gory monster of the centuries. It is deaf to reason and to all appeals upon grounds of justice, equity and the high principles of righteousness and mercy, which are the only true bases of a just government. Christianity, like other religions, stands appalled in its massive shadow and quails before its grim visage. It denies and despises "the brotherhood of man and the fatherhood of God," even while it professes the religion of the lowly Nazarene. The force of arms, the triumph of conquering armies, the commands and edicts of governments neither destroy nor control its savage nature nor reduce the plenitude of its power.

Not only does prejudice lead to oppression, the subversion of justice and right, but there is nothing more serious and more in evidence than the fact that there is a vast legalized scheme throughout the South to set the iron heel more permanently and desperately upon the head of the black man as a race, and as individual characters. There would be hope to the rejected and aspiring Afro-American if good character and becoming behavior would or could count for anything in the civic arena. But we are now confronted by conditions where merit in the black man does not weigh one iota in human rights, and very little in human life, if that life and character is under a black or brown skin. Learning, personal accomplishments, the achievement of wealth, the reign of morality, and skilled handicraft amount to nothing whatever in the black man. Merit and fitness for citizenship and advanced qualifications for the high and holy functions of civil life cannot win for him the rights and safety that is the natural and God-given inheritance of all. Nowhere in the South is the black man as safe in his person and property as is the white man. No negro can feel the same assurance of protection and safety, even in the absence of the mob, as those of the opposite or ruling race. The laws and police regulations are one thing to the white people, but quite another thing to the black people.

Black men and black women, though cultured and refined, are treated as serfs and subjected to every imaginable insult and degradation that can be invented or discovered by an ill-plighted and perverse ingenuity.

But especially do we see and feel the power of oppression in the construction and operation of the laws and that sentiment that gave them birth and execution, and which is stronger, more exacting than the written laws themselves. Ever since President Hayes had his seat in the White House, when the State governments reverted to the control of the original South, step by step, the legislative enactments have drawn the cords of discrimination and oppression with increasing stringency and an intensifying vindictiveness that seem phenomenal and inhuman. If by these methods of oppression and hardship entailed on black citizens anything could be gained or added to the happiness and prosperity of the dominant people, there might be some reason or cause for its existence. No morals are to be improved by it, no greater degree of polished manners is to be achieved, and nothing but self-debauchment to the oppressor and degradation to the oppressed are to be gained. And since there is nothing to be gained, it is evident that the only object in view is to oppress and destroy the progress and development of the Afro-American people, a people who have never sought to do them a wrong or an injury. The desire on their part is to make negro freedom and possibilities a total and signal failure, and defeat the ends of a better negro manhood, and prove as true the oft-repeated assertion that "the black race is incapable of rising to the dignity of a full-fledged common citizenship." They believe that it is wrong to educate the negroes beyond a small degree of handicraft, suitable only for the most menial service and the smallest wages.

It is a fact, now universally known and acknowledged, that the political rights and privileges conferred on the black race by the general government have been totally and irretrievably annihilated in almost every part of the South. Where they have failed in total destruction of these rights by direct legislation, they have annulled them by a system of evasions and subterfuges. The votes of black citizens are no longer factors of consideration in the political equation, and they are shorn of all those sacred functions and agencies by which the highest and best citizenship is attained. This not only helps to degrade and destroy legitimate aspiration and subverts the operating faculties of respectable and decent manhood, but reduces the millions of the black race to a growing and enlarging system of serfdom and political peonage that is but a little short of abject slavery. Neither does it appear that there is any remedy or appeal by which these flagrant wrongs and perversions of civil rights can be adjusted and made to comply with the demands of true American citizenship. It may be stated as axiomatic, *that no people can advance in true American citizenship and reach high moral and political ideals in the functions and practices of the franchise, when they are excluded from it and from those responsibilities that must follow its exercise.* The destruction of a "free ballot and a fair count" not only destroys the national guarantee of protection, of liberty, person and property, but must prove in the end a threatening calamity to the Federal compact of States and dangerous to the freedom of its citizens. In the South the millions of black people are denied this guarantee of protection to life, liberty and property, with no hope or chance of redress. There is no appeal, unless from Caesar to Caesar, which is equivalent to no appeal at all. At the same time the general government does nothing to defend and preserve its great and majestic acts of sovereign right embodied in the Constitution of the United States, but allows the evil to fasten its grip upon all the States of the South.

This puts the negro race not only in a state of semi-serfdom, but the methods employed and the efforts to further submerge the natural and political rights of negro manhood grow apace as the days go by. How, then, can the Afro-American rise to the dignity of good citizenship and aspire to its possibilities, when political rights, privileges and agencies are taken from him? Can he make bricks without straw, or do the impossible? Indeed, he is in a deplorable condition, from whatever standpoint we view the situation.

It has been supposed by most of the leading negro men, as well as many philanthropic friends in the North, that whenever the negro is prepared for the duties and responsibilities of citizenship, by culture, wealth and moral standing, and that whenever he becomes a skilled artisan and scientific farmer, then as a race the white people of the South will bestow upon him equal political privileges with themselves. And thus it is claimed that a certain sort of education and training is calculated to settle the problem of the races. At first glimpse this seems a fair presumption, and maybe it ought to be so, and we heartily wish that it might so result. But experience contradicts it and leaves us hopeless of obtaining the rights and privileges of suffrage and cognate rights of citizenship.

To make this clearer, no man of color, no matter how cultured and worthy, or however accomplished, refined and fitted, has ever been allowed to occupy the same civic plane with the white man of the South for a single hour. In this respect Bishop Turner, Frederick Douglass, or Dr. Booker T. Washington has no more chance than the most degraded of our race. It would approximate a small riot should such negro celebrities attempt to enter a hotel or public resort, assuming the airs of equality on the civic plane. Hence all negroes are excluded from positions and places of lucrative employment, with the irrevocable negation, "No negroes are wanted." He may be better prepared than the white applicant, but prejudice forbids the black race to enter. As the black man of the South approximates the standard of Anglo-Saxon civic life in its best phases and highest standard of excellence, race feelings, antagonisms, and antipathies will increase in bitterness, extent and intensity. And this will be so as long as one race is white and the other black, both occupying the same physical territory.

There is no force or power, apparently, at command to regulate and harmonize diverse elements and social agencies so dissimilar as are seen in the racial phase of the body politic. As long as the negro is a black man, and as long as the opposite individual is a white man, so long must the social factors and political entities war against each other.

Race traits and race peculiarities are the natural and enduring faculties that prolong the war and the bitter strife of inharmonious relations.

It is true, legally allowed amalgamation would settle all racial difficulties by the natural process of absorption and disintegration of racial characteristics, but that is a thing unthinkable, unlegalizable and beyond the realms of debate. It is undeniable that amalgamation is going on in the South, and legal marriages to some extent in the North; but in both sections of the country it is slow, while the products of the same are rejected by the ruling race to the same extent as the typical negro. Where it is illegal it is a crime, and conflicts with the code of decency and morality. It debauches the moral sense and destroys the purity and dignity of young negro motherhood, and debases both sexes in their moral natures. Legal intermarriage in the South, although not wrong in its consummation, is a matter as yet undebatable, and belongs only to the future.

But comparing the present situation with the history of Anglo-Saxon life, we see no chance for the negro race to hold its identity of racial traits and characteristics, while the percentage of Negro blood infused into Anglo-Saxon veins is too small to change, to any perceptible degree, the distinctive features of visible or physical character.

As long as the two races live in the same territory in immediate contact, their relations will be such as to intermingle to that degree where "half-bloods," quarter-bloods, and a mongrel progeny will result. This is not only going on now, but is destined to annihilate the true typical antebellum negro type, and put in his place a stronger, a longer lived, and a more Anglo-Saxon-like, homogeneous race. In other words, the negro to come will not be the negro of the emancipation proclamation, but he will be the Anglo-Saxonized Afro-American. It seems true, as has been said, "No race can look the Anglo-Saxon in the face and live." Certainly no other race can hold its own in his immediate presence. Being in immediate contact, and underrating the mental and moral virtues of others and exercising a sovereignty over them, his opportunities are enlarged to make other races his own in consanguinity. This he never fails to do.

It is often said the difficulties, growing out of the race problem, would be greatly reduced in enormity if the negro would remain in the rural districts and on the farms. At first view this assertion seems to accord with reason, common sense and the best interest of the race. Certainly it appears that such conditions are the best for the negro masses, and most promotive of moral and physical health, as well as advancement in social and material economics. Indeed, it is to be regretted, if not lamented, that great masses of negroes leave the country districts and farms and herd and cluster in the towns and cities. But since this is done, there must be some real cause for it, a cause that enters deeply into the interest and material welfare. Neither is it strange when we consider the fact that in the country or rural districts of the South, no negro, or at best few negroes, feel safe in their person and property. Often they are ruthlessly and unnecessarily insulted, abused, lynched, killed, or driven from their homes without the slightest hope of protection or redress. Often their mothers, sisters and daughters are corrupted and debauched almost before their eyes, yet nothing is done to stop the wicked and nefarious practice or bring to punishment the evil doer. Besides wages are small, and in many instances are a mere pittance to keep soul and body together. Of course, there are some honorable exceptions, but they are few and far between.

The school system in the country is a mere shadow and a real farce. The very fact that negroes in great masses leave the country and resort to towns and cities shows an unrest and a fervid disquietude that rest upon apprehension and real cause. Even those who have been able to procure homes of their own, along with other substantial belongings, are in a state of uneasiness and mental perturbation. They do not know how soon they may be falsely accused by some trifling and envious white man and lynched by the cruel and bloody mob. For as soon as the black man in the rural districts gets a home with a farm attached and reaches a state of prosperity, then the jealousies of the white people are aroused and excited, and the prosperous negro is watched and criticised. Here the conflict of opposite races begins and ends in total defeat for the black man. Indeed, there is little or no chance for the black man in the country if he grows rich, polished, and puts on style, or tries to be equal to the white neighbor in civic attainments. Good breeding, politeness, kindness, self-respect and all the virtues may be added and retained by a black man, as have been attained by many, but these, instead of helping him to live in the esteem of his white neighbor, actually put him in a precarious condition, and endangers his life and property. Thus we see, from this view, there is absolutely no chance for the negro race in the country districts to live and prosper without a state of incertitude and unrest.

It approximates the largest truth as well as covers the most dogmatic and momentous phase of this great question that now confronts and perplexes us, when we say that *two distinct peoples can never live together in the South in peace, when the one is Anglo-Saxon and the other negro, unless the negro, as a race or en masse, lives in the submerged realm of serfdom and slavery.*

It is true, there is room enough in territorial extent; there is abundance of water, sky and land, but on the social and political plane there is not room enough for both races as civil equals. The white people of the South have not been willing in the past; they are less willing now, and reason and experience teach us that they will not be willing at any time in the endless future for the race of black men to become their political equals, or occupy the same plane of freedom and citizenship, with themselves, no matter how well qualified they may be for it. It is folly, if not idiotic, unless the supernatural intervenes, of which we have promise, to expect it at all.

One of the most far-reaching and fatal attributes of the great problem, now considered, is the constant and wide-spread practice of debauching the young motherhood of the negro race by the ruling people. Perhaps there is nothing connected with a life of a race so damaging and destructive to its morals, mental expansion and physical development as to have its mothers corrupted and despoiled of their procreative sanctity. It can but beget a race of weaklings and effeminates in moral, mental and physical health. How a people are to become wise, upright and healthy in body and mind while their mothers, daughters and sisters are polluted in their genital powers is hard to see. As like begets like, and as criminals beget criminals, and as the parent is reflected and duplicated in the natural offsprings, so the race, thus corrupted by miscegenation and clandestine production, must ride to its downfall and racial dissolution. It does not help the case to argue that the black women ought to resist, or that their virtue ought to be a guarantee of successful resistance against attack. True, it ought to be so, and yet it was never so. But environments and conditions have much to do with it. Wisdom and philanthropy would suggest that the best situation be assumed and the best conditions arranged so as to make the resisting power stronger by diminishing the opportunities of the advancing foe.

But a serious phase and a damaging factor of this question are the constant and universal tendency in the South to gradually reduce the great bulk of the negro race to a state of serfdom and peonage. So usual and constant is the progressive work of this form of degradation and oppression that even negroes themselves seem to accept it as a matter of course, or as what is expected, while philanthropic people have no knowledge of it, or in some way pass it by unheeded. None but those who have lived and traveled through the rural districts of the South and made it a study can enter its many-threaded details, and comprehend the subtle and evasive methods by which the negroes are kept at the lowest ebb of civil life. It is in the small details of every-day life, with the customs, sentiment and tendencies, by which the true state of the race is seen in connection with the ruling people. Prejudice, discrimination and double dealing crop out in almost every business transaction. White men expect to be treated differently from black men, while black men never expect to be treated with the same degree of civility as white people receive. There is one code of morals and civil ethics for the white-skinned man and another for the black-skinned man, with the heaviest of its iron hand resting upon the head of the black man, on his children and his civilization, if civilization it be. It is both terrible and monstrous, and perhaps the greatest phenomenon of the whole racial problem, that black men, or any other race of men, would or could stand quietly by and neglect the opportunities of the golden hour to throw off the yoke and repel the smiting hand that enwreathes and rivets the heavy steel upon their necks. Even evasions and the signalizing and the ponderous stroke of universal aversion are neglected, and the slow death is left in the coils of the always forging links and lengthening chains of a second form of old slavery. There are those who believe that the South can and ought to be allowed to settle the race problem in her own way. For this she clamors and pleads to be "let alone." The white people of the South vehemently declare that they can settle it, and we do not doubt their willingness and ability to do so. But how? Where will the black man stand if he stands at all? Let the history of the great past and the transactions of the present answer.

To allow the South to settle this great question in its own way simply means to degrade the black race and remand and doom the black people to an inexorable peonage and eternal serfdom. The proposition is utterly incompatible with reason and what should be expected. Colleges and schools of high grade, and such enabling facilities of human development would become obsolete, and a liberal and substantial cultural process, that alone can develop a people, will become things of the past, known only as facts of an historic age.

The great majority of the Southern white people hold that education ruins the negro, and especially the higher education or collegiate training, and more especially under Northern white teachers. They make the claim that it unfits him for usefulness and that kind of citizenship that belongs to him as an inferior. Anything that takes the black man from the ditch, the cane farm or the cotton field as a mere menial laborer, as a "hewer of wood and drawer of water," is adverse to his best estate, God-given and ordained, and whoever, therefore, attempts to do it, or whoever succeeds or partially succeeds in doing so, is the negro's greatest enemy and a giant foe to the South; that the friend of the negro is absolutely and necessarily an enemy of the South. This is so absurd, and contrary to fact, reason and history that it requires no serious attempt for signal and complete contradiction. Education and training help every creature to fulfill better the ends of being and the onerous duties of life. The trained horse, the cultured dog, the domiciled and domesticated animals are all made better and more useful in their operating sphere by the cultural process. Why not the negro? Is he any less than the beast of the field?

But the South cannot settle this problem any more than it could settle the long and bloody problem of slavery. In the very nature of the case it is a national question, a question too big for the South. It belongs before the bar of the whole nation. Even if it were not national in its scope and depth, the South would be an incompetent juror, because she is not willing for all of her people, black and white, to enjoy equal privileges and rights, even when given by the central government. Such a juror could not render an impartial verdict.

Again, it is national because none but the nation has the strong hand and fullness of power competent to meet the issue and adjust relations. Then, again, it involves national honor and national law. Neither can it rest where it is. It is an historic as well as a philosophical truism that no question in government can be settled until it is settled right. It must be settled right in the native fundamentals and cohesive elements and faculties. All of the people must be free and allowed to enjoy their natural and lawful rights, or else the conflict must and will continue. So long as there is a part of the people oppressed and denied the rights and privileges of citizenship that is designed to be universal and applicable to all, the problem cannot be settled. It cannot be settled any more than the question of slavery could have been settled, leaving the slaves in slavery. Slavery, which stood and towered and lifted its hideous form, dripping with the innocent blood of the slave, stood for awhile in the emblazoned arena of American liberty, but it fell and sent the tremor of its fall through the approaching decades, with whose blighting shadow we are fighting to-day! And until right triumphs and oppression and wrong cease, the unity of truth and the reign of God forbid a cessation of hostilities.

But, as we see no chance for the black man to arrive at his best and highest possibilities and the noble ends of the best citizenship in the same territory with the white people of the South, segregation is proposed as the best, the most practicable and desirable method in the solution of the racial problem. Black men are as much citizens of the American federation of States as white men. They should never rest or cease legitimate efforts until full and plenipotent citizenship is given to them, the same as white men. They should contend for it as the dearest, as the highest privilege, and the most sacred part of their national inheritance! If the white people of the South would accord to the African people the full measure of citizenship with themselves, allowing them to live upon the same plane of civil life, we could ask no more, and the racial problem would cease to be a problem. But since this is not done, and since it seems to be clear that it will not be done, then we ask for a settlement of our racial troubles by separation and segregation of the races in the South, at least.

We ask for a State or States, or a Territory, or a part or parts of Territories within the limits of the United States, our great country. To reach these ends, the following propositions may be considered within the limits of possibilities:

I. There is a great problem growing out of the fact that two distinct races or peoples are occupying the same territory under the same government and laws; that they are so distinct and dissimilar in racial traits, instincts and character, that it is impossible for them to live together on equal terms of social and political relation, or on terms of equal citizenship.

II. The problem of the races is inter-racial and national, affecting the entire country in its vast interests, prosperity and progress. And, therefore, it is the duty of the general government to settle it, as that is the only power that can do it.

III. The segregation of the races is the most practicable, logical, and equitable solution of the problem.

IV. Segregation and separation should be gradual and classified by a qualified citizenship, and non-compulsory, so as not to injure or retard labor, capital, and commerce in those States where the negro is an important factor of production and consumption.

V. To make the movement operative and effective, the negro population of the Southern States should send petitions to the President and the Congress of the United States of America asking for segregation. They should ask for suitable territory in the great republic, as legal and equal citizens of the Union, and not go out of their country to be exposed to doubtful experiment and foreign complications. Afro-Americans should remain in their own country, and in the zone of greatness, and in the latitude of progress.

VI. The government would, providing segregation materializes, establish and maintain suitable laws, regulations, and safe grounds for the maintenance of the civil order, peace, progress, and prosperity.

VII. The place or places, or the territory may be

selected by competent authority from the western part of the public domain, such as a part of the Indian Territory, New Mexico, or other parts of the great West.

VIII. No white person or persons should be allowed to obtain citizenship in such a State or Territory, unless identified with the negro race by marriage, and those who may be appointed by the government to expedite and control the Federal interests, provided also that the general public have the same privileges, rights, protection and safety in the segregated Territory as in the other States of the Union.

IX. There should be some easy and practical qualifications required of those who are to become citizens of the segregated Territory. They should have, at least, a reputable character, some degree of education, and perhaps a competency for one year's support. Criminals and undesirable persons should be kept out, as far as possible, until they are properly qualified to meet the requirements.

It may be said and will be said that it will be impossible to keep the white man out and the black man in. But let it be remembered that the object is not to keep the white man out or the black man in, but to establish a State or States in which alone the Afro-American people may dominate by eligibility to political office, the public trust and control; thus conferring upon them all the rights of full and free citizenship enjoyed by others, and which is denied them in the Southern States.

Of course, citizens of all States would be free to come and go, but none to acquire citizenship unless identified with the negro race. Afro-Americans have no desire, as a race, to create friction, antagonisms and strife, but ask and demand at this time the rights and privileges authorized by the government.

It is to be admitted that the plan of segregation here

presented is environed and beset with many difficulties. We realize the stern fact that any plan to settle the racial problem, which may be presented, will have not only its difficulties, but its objectors. But any plan which may be proposed for the solution of the question cannot be surrounded nor carry more difficulties and perplexities than the present state and condition of the races. No plan or method of solution can produce more bitterness, alienation, degradation, bloodshed and death than the present state of affairs.

But especially will it be urged by friends as well as by the enemies of the Afro-American people that the negro is incapable of self-government and control. But how do they know? Where has it ever been tried under conditions that may be obtained within the Federal Union? Besides, if the government of the United States cannot control and direct a few millions of its citizens who may be segregated for the peaceful solution of a great national problem, it would be too weak and ephemeral to hold its parts together. The idea is preposterous and fallacious in the extreme.

Not only has the negro some degree of American civilization engrafted upon his progressive and developing manhood, but he has a large and increasing percentage of Anglo-Saxon blood in his veins, and consequently Anglo-Saxon life. He is not only patriotic and devoted to his country, but the trend of events and the stern logic of fact and principle show him to be capable of civilization and susceptible of being wrought into the social and political compact. What is most needed for his development is a chance to be a man, an open door for his possibilities.

It is often affirmed in the South that "this is a white man's country." This is freely admitted, but it is equally true that it is also the black man's country. The country belongs to every man born on its soil, black or white. If it is the white man's country in any supreme or particular sense, it furnishes an important reason why he should be just and humane to all, most especially to under-graduates in civil life.

It may be argued that many Southern people will oppose the separation of the races upon the ground that such would destroy the labor element of the South and thus retard expansion and progress. This may be or will be found to be true in some degree, but it is becoming more and more evident that negro labor is growing less important as a factor of production in the South. It is not now more than one-half of the labor employed in field and shop. A large proportion of it has gone North, East and West, and is still going, until ere long the great black belts of the South must be numbered with the things of the past.

As a laborer in the South, the negro has been the dearest and most expensive that a country has ever had in the history of nations. The Southern people have already paid an enormous price for the negro as a slave, and still the astounding debt bears interest, compounding itself as the years go by. Heaps of gold and almost endless treasure have been paid for his blood and bones as a labor element. Brave sons, noble sires, and intrepid chieftains, queenly women, with the flower of the land have been slain upon its high places. Millions of drops of blood have been poured out as a bloody libation at the shrine of the swarthy Moloch. And it seems apparent that the union of States that has cost so much will never be one with a tenacious integrity until black Ham and white Japheth shall dwell in separate tents.

In a State to themselves, within the Federal Union, the negro would become a free and full-fledged citizen, with all the immunities, privileges and political rights that belong to American citizens without friction, envy and jealousies. Then the negro, as a man and a race, would have a chance to develop his mental powers, his physical character, and his essential responsibilities as an American citizen. The responsibilities that would come with a degree of self-government would inspire, qualify and stimulate to supreme effort in life, and thus help the Anglo-Saxon man and brother to carry his great civilization to a higher plane and a loftier altitude of ideal perfection.

Indeed, the Union of the States will never be fully and perfectly recemented with tenacious integrity until black Ham and white Japheth dwell together in separate tents.

BURDEN OF THE NEGRO PROBLEM.

BY RICHARD H. EDMONDS,
Editor "Manufacturers' Record."

Chief of the burdens of the negro problem is the heed given to words of exploiters of the negro.

As long as the intelligence of the country fails to dicountenance the discussion of the negro by professional orators, Chautauqua or lyceum lecturers, educationalists, confirmed philanthropists and designing politicians who find therein more or less personal profit, so long will the difficulties of the problem persist.

Could it be left to men of the character, the standing, the experience, the mental calibre and the common sense of Stuyvesant Fish, of New York; T. G. Bush, of Alabama; William A. Courtenay, of South Carolina; John L. Williams, of Virginia; D. A. Tompkins, of North Carolina; J. B. Killebrew, of Tennessee; W. J. Northen, of Georgia, and John H. Kirby, of Texas, the happy solution of the problem could be offered in a trice.

Fundamentally it is, as it has always been, an economic problem to be dealt with, not in ignorance, prejudice or passion, but in knowledge, wisdom and judgment, and in sober conviction of responsibility to the white race and to the black. Essentially there should be an attitude toward the negro no whit different from that toward the hordes of aliens that are crowding into the country through its eastern ports. The latter are really the more difficult to be handled, in that they have never had the negro's advantage of contact with American whites of pure stock. Their future as affecting for good or ill the history of this land is inextricably involved with the future of the negro as he shall be hampered or helped.

As the negro is mistreated or is unimpeded in working out his own career, the menace in foreign fugitives from oppression or poverty will wax or wane. To the extent that the South shall be relieved from the unnecessary embarrassments in negro development, to that extent will the South be free to aid more unfortunate parts of the country solving their more ponderous problems.

Alternatives proposed as solutions of the negro problem are amalgamation, annihilation, deportation, Each means mistreatment of the negro; each is impracticable.

Deportation was tried forty years ago under conditions where alone it could approach possibility. At the instigation of Abraham Lincoln attempt was made to supplement emancipation with exodus, under government auspices. It failed signally in an odor of graft. Of the hundred thousand dollars available for the experiment, the account rendered of two or three years' expenditures was for about thirty-three thousand dollars, the bulk of which had gone to agents, with a government vessel sent to bring back a handful of colonists who had been induced to go to another land. If the plan could not but fail for four million negroes with Lincoln as a leading promoter, at a time when the Constitution of the country was in abeyance, why should sanity consider it to-day when more than eight million negroes are to be taken into account, in addition to the whites or the whole country?

The negro is doing too much for the prosperity of the country for him to desire to leave it or for the whites to give encouragement to anybody who would force or persuade him to leave.

Amalgamation has within itself the elements of its own destruction. Miscegenation carries with it its own punishment. Its effects are reducing to the minimum the number of whites and blacks who will submit to it.

Some of the members of that race, seething with the passions in which they were begotten, are openly or covertly leading a few negroes to inevitable ruin with themselves. Extremists among the amalgamates may in the course of time subject themselves to deportation to penal settlements or to more speedy ends at the hands of the law or outside the law, while a rapidly growing sentiment in favor of a humane surgical operation, to be added to the punishment of the penitentiary, will, to a certain degree, annihilate a part of the negro stock by making it incapable of propagation. This, enforced as to criminal whites as well as to criminal negroes, would not only have a deterrent influence to prevent crime, but it would gradually lessen the reproduction of criminals. But it is puerile and cowardly to talk of annihilating a people who, interrupted by force, and practically without action on their own part, in their reasonable, healthy development forty years ago, and since then the victims of experiments that would have crippled forever almost any race, have more than doubled in number and still display traces of the excellent education of their race made possible in the change from slavery in Africa to bondage in America.

A suggestion of comparatively recent publicity is that negro vexations be overcome by opening the gates to Mongolian labor. There is a charm about that for the economic politician, in that the element in American politics that is largely responsible for the ills of the negro, created in the use of him as a political issue to crystalize the low order intellect of voters in close elections, is most strenuous for Chinese exclusion. That element may be gagged against negro agitation by the threat of Chinese agitation. But that would be politics; and there has been already too much politics about the negro. Statesmanship is demanded, and statésmanship will not jump from the frying pan into the fire.

Statesmanship sees a solution of the negro problem in removing the obstacles from the way of the development of the negro's aptitude, and in encouraging him in cultivation of those habits which have become second nature with the white race for its advancement.

Such a policy recognizes these facts emphasized by the experience of the past forty years.

The negro race is not the Caucasian race merely colored black.

The negro race, mentally and morally, is centuries behind the Caucasian and has never given evidence of ability to advance in that respect of its own initiative.

Crossed upon white stock the negro is given greater mental strength, but a strength likely to be exerted in manifestation of the vices rather than of the virtues of the original stocks.

The negro race, physically, is a powerful race, and fit to work under proper guidance.

To seek to give the negro child, but three centuries removed from the jungle, the start in schooling similar to that given the white child, with a thousand years of the education of individual effort behind it, was worse than foolhardy. It was not unlike placing a loaded magazine rifle in the arms of a chimpanzee.

To give the negro male the ballot, a privilege won by the white man in centuries of struggle and, after all, not always exercised in a manner justifying his victory, was worse than criminal. It was not unlike poisoning a stream at its very source.

Like education for whites and blacks, education without distinction of race, are the baneful theories which, applied for nearly two generations, have not only injured the negro in weaning him from incentives to productive and beneficial exertions into sloth, vice and crime, but have even twisted the training of whites upon right lines. In forcing the suffrage upon the negro there was injected into the whole body politic a virus of corruption in party practices and in municipal, State and national administrations flatly disproving much of the theory of public education.

It is but a step from mendicant methods in negro education to mendicant methods in white education. Such pauperization is but the fertilization of the soil of graft in quarters high and low. So, the negro problem belongs to us all. The intelligence and patriotism of the whole country must combine for its solution, in permitting the South, most affected by it at present, to determine the way and supply the means. Broad, well-defined principles must guide us.

Efforts to educate the rising generation of negroes must recognize, for avoidance, the mistakes of the past manifested by negro youth of to-day. Expenditures of time, energy and money must be per capacity of the negro instead of per capita.

Negroes who have been miseducated must be brought back to the proper starting point before it is too late. They must not only be allowed in other parts of the country the opportunities to work enjoyed by them in the South, but they must be sharply taught that unless they work they will starve. The machinery for such instruction is to be had in a stringent vagrancy law, enforced completely by an effective rural police or patrol, with provision that individuals who will not work for themselves and for others shall be forced to work for the State in fields not conflicting with honest labor.

The way must be kept open for the natural diffusion of the negroes among the white population until they become an element inconsequential from the social, political or any other standpoint. At present there is one negro for every 8.6 of the total population of the country. That ratio would be a safe one if it was common to all parts of the country. But it is not. In the South there is one negro for every three of the population, the ratio ranging from one in twenty-two in West Virginia to 1 in 1.7 in Mississippi and South Carolina. At the same time in the fifteen States east of the Mississippi and north of the Ohio and Mason and Dixon line, the proportion is 1 negro for every 55.2 of the population, the range being from 1 in 6 in Deleware to 1 in 621 in New Hampshire. In the eleven mountain and Pacific states the proportion is 1 in 163, and in 9 other States and territories it is 1 in 36.

As long as any distinct race is massed in one section of the country, so long will that race be hampered and so long will it be a drag upon the whole country.

The politician, the sensation monger or any other individual in any part of the country who, in using the negro for every other purpose but the negro's good, retards the natural diffusion of the negro revealed in the fact that near 1,000,000 negroes are now living outside the South in a total of 8,834,000, is an enemy to his country and must be suppressed. Those who would suppress him have only to bear in mind the significant fact that the race question is invariably brought to the front when the leading political parties of the country lack the courage to formulate and support policies appealing to the intelligence of the people, or when the movement carrying more negroes to other parts of the country and more whites to the South is most pronounced.

Of all persons, Southern men should have no part in giving life to negro agitation. The negro is in this country for good. We must meet this situation not with impracticable theories, supported by overdrawn pictures of danger from his presence. No reasonable man could, with prophetic sight, have viewed the influences exerted upon negroes for forty years without expecting even more trouble than we have had. Suddenly freed from the restraining power which had controlled and civilized them, taught by the most unscrupulous white scoundrels that ever cursed a land, as well as by misguided philanthropists from other sections, that they must demand social equality, who could expect aught but a generation of criminal instincts. But this criminality is less than might have been anticipated. Upon the white people of the South rests the responsibility of being permitted to deal with infinite patience with a race, millions of which have proved that they could be honest, virtuous, hard working and faithful to every trust. The demons in human shape whose horrible acts are followed by swift punishment, which, however severe, can never be severe enough to atone for the crime, should not arouse resentment against the whole race. The mad dog is a terror, but the fact that some dogs go mad is never taken as a sufficient reason for driving every dog out of the country.

The negro is with us, and he is going to stay with us. How shall we get the best for him and for ourselves out of the situation? Not by deportation, not by amalgamation, but by the same tireless work which the South has for forty years given to this question, freed, however, from the visionary theories of outsiders, who know nothing about the conditions in the South, and the equally visionary theories of impracticable Southern men. With the marked increase of white immigration to the South now under way, the tendency of the negroes to dispersion throughout the country, the enactment and enforcement of vagrancy laws, the establishment of country patrol systems, and the gradual elimination of the criminal classes in reproduction, the negro question will no longer afford profitable employment for public speakers and magazine writers.

A SOLUTION OF THE NEGRO PROBLEM PSYCHOLOGICALLY CONSIDERED.

By WILLIS B. PARKS, M.D.

In this treatise it is proposed to present the negro problem in its various aspects, on a different basis and from a different standpoint from that which it has hitherto been treated. It will be shown that the existing conditions are the logical and unfailing consequence of cause and effect. This question is by no means local or sectional, but is universal in its scope and application. It is, therefore, not a Southern problem that we are dealing with, but a national one, far-reaching and vast.

The most important part of man is mind, and, therefore, any treatment of the negro problem that ignores that faculty, is lacking from a philosophical viewpoint. Hudson truly says, "The laws of suggestion are the most important factor of man's make-up." Hence it is to that faculty that a scientific inquiry must address itself. In using the expression "suggestion," it is not the intention to mystify, but rather to simplify. It is obvious that there are several kinds of suggestions, and that they are different in their manifestations, but from whatever source they emanate, they are subject to the same fixed laws. We recognize direct as well as indirect suggestions, and suggestions may be conscious and unconscious.

To illustrate: When the negro was freed and given the right of suffrage, he was given the indirect suggestion of social equality; to receive him into the family and give him the best room in the house, would be a direct suggestion of social equality. To give the negro advantages of education and then not to find a niche to fit him in after life, is also to give him the suggestion of equality, but, at the same time, to prepare him for ultimate and grievous disappointment.

In the light of the above illustrations, the term Auto-Suggestion might also be understood. The old slave negro had the idea of slavery so indelibly impressed upon him, that nothing else suggested itself, from this view-point, to him, and so, even after he had been freed, the before-the-war negro acts now and talks like a slave, and is most comfortable in that condition.

Another very important point, with reference to suggestion, is to be observed, namely, that it can be both given and received unconsciously. Moreover, it may be given consciously and received unconsciously.

Finally, it should be understood that suggestion, when directly received or when suddenly aroused to new life and called into activity after existing long in a dormant state, is not a weakling attribute of man's nature. It becomes a power, moving with resistless force and dominating the will with such energy as to sometimes override every opposing influence, transform the being and strike down all opposition to his sway.

What better illustration than the mob? Here we see suggestion playing upon the passions of men, until reason becomes dethroned, for the once peaceable, quiet and law-respecting citizens become a maddened mass of death-dealing animals. Men who would not only scorn to strike a foe when he is down, but who would succor the imperiled even at the risk of life itself, become forgetful of every rational influence, and join in the taking of the life of a helpless human being.

And this is a fair illustration. The thought of summary punishment may have originated in a single mind—auto-suggestive—but how quickly suggestion, conscious, direct, is imparted from the lips or by a flash of the eyes, or by a gesture from one to another, until, in a trice, the first mutterings of the storm have gathered such force that it has become a whirling, seething cyclone of wrath, and impaled within the vortex of its fury, writhes the doomed victim.

Let it be at last remembered, that the negro was brought here in a state of savagery and ignorance and subjected to the suggestions, conscious and unconscious, of a highly organized civilization. It is with these things in view that we propose to treat this subject, under the following heads: The Semi-Savage Negro; The Slave Negro; The Ex-Slave Negro; The New Negro.

THE SEMI-SAVAGE NEGRO.

Historically, about 290 years ago the negro was brought from Africa in a semi-savage condition to the United States. The object being not to civilize him, but to enslave him. It was purely from mercenary motives, and not on account of a desire to elevate him from a barbaric state and civilize and enlighten and Christianize him.

At first, the negro did not prove profitable in the hands of his masters. The cold climate of the Northern States of the Union, where he was first domiciled, was too rigorous for the thin-skinned Africans, and the great majority of them were later transferred to Southern territory, where not only the climate suited them the best, but they were best adapted to the field culture of the section.

Thus the new importation proved valueless to the original importers, except as a speculative commodity. But in his new home he rapidly became domesticated, and the imitative being a strong faculty of his nature, he was enabled soon to adapt himself to his surroundings, and he proved a ready learner to do work of a more or less simple character. Indeed, his progress was more rapid along this line than was his mental development; hence, the negro was a first-rate field hand before his jargon became barely intelligible. And, as an illustration of the tardiness of the negro as a linguist, it is only necessary to refer to the low-country negro (as the Southern people term him) on the rice plantations of the South, and along the whole south coasts. Their feeble vocabulary of English is so interspersed with their own peculiar jargon, half English and half barbaric, as to render it unintelligible, except to one long used to hearing it.

It is this creature, in his new surroundings; simple, pliable and peculiarly susceptible to whatever influences that are brought to bear upon his untutored mind, that we shall undertake to deal with, from a psychological view-point.

According to Hudson, a recognized authority upon psychology, every human being is endowed with a dual mind; the objective, or the reasoning mind is "controlled by the five senses (seeing, hearing, feeling, etc.); it is the outgrowth of man's physical necessities. It is his guide in his struggles with material environment. Its highest function is that of reasoning."

"The Subjective takes cognizance," says the same authority, "of its environments by means independent of the five physical senses. It perceives by intuition. It is the seat of the emotions, and the storehouse of memory, etc." This duality of the mind renders man susceptible to all kinds of suggestions known to the realms of psychology. Boris Sidis says, "The soil favorable for the seeds of suggestion exists in all individuals. The suggestible element is a constituent of our nature—it never leaves us."

The following will illustrate the manner in which suggestion is received by the subjective mind in a normal, or waking, state. Before, or when such suggestion finds lodgment, the ideas and beliefs existing, that have come through the objective mind, and that are antagonistic to such suggestion, must be overcome. If the subject be in a hypnotic state the objective mind is passive, and the suggestion is imparted, direct, to the subjective, without having to overcome the objective mind, i. e., the auto-suggestion that already exists. And as it is while in the normal or waking state of the negro, only, that we propose to deal with the subject, the sleeping or hypnotic side of psychology or suggestion will receive no further consideration.

THE SLAVE NEGRO.

With the advancement of the slavery period the negro progressed even more rapidly than might have been expected along many lines. He became more and more desirable as a servant, and, correspondingly, his money value was enhanced. He was, as a rule, the recipient of humane treatment; his food was plentiful and wholesome, his clothing comfortable, and when sick he was provided with the best medical treatment. His money value demanded all this, even if the demand came from no higher or more humane motives. But soon there did arise a bond of sympathy between master and slave—call it affection if you please— that widened and deepened as the years passed; and this bond, so subtle as to elude the grasp of poet and philosopher alike, who would portray its character, survived, even after the slave became a freedman, and although suggestion, of a baleful and poisonous character, promptly followed the emancipation of the slaves, uprooting and destroying much of that feeling existing between the races, yet it still lingers in the breasts of many of the ex-slaves of to-day, and, certainly, there is a feeling of tender regard in the hearts of their former masters for those who were once their slaves.

During the existence of slavery the surroundings, the occupation, the every environment of the negro strengthened, each day, the first and only conscious suggestion of the relation of the races, the one toward the other, in the mind of the negro—that of master and slave. There was a gulf, deep and impassable, fixed by the laws of nature, and illustrated in the color of the skin of each race, that separated them as completely and effectually, socially, as if the breadth of a continent lay between.

The slave negro realized this, accepted it, and lived up to the conditions. And, even after the President of the United States in 1863 had issued his emancipation proclamation, and all the world waited in breathless expectancy for the blow, so strongly suggested in that document, to fall, that would inaugurate a reign of bloodshed, butchery and rapine all over the South, the terrors of which men could not conceive of, this principle, so well grounded by suggestion in the conscience of these slaves, stayed the hand, and palsied the arm of any that might have contemplated the dreadful uprising, and, in the hands of the black man, the lives and homes of the women and children, whose slave he was, were a sacred charge, and not an act of lawlessness mars the black man's history during that dark period. What an illustration of right suggestion!

And who shall say that, left to themselves, uninfluenced by conscious counter suggestions coming from designing and insincere persons, whose sole object was personal gain and political preference, the conditions of to-day would have been the same? But the fire once ignited, conditions were such as to fan the flame into intense heat at once, and suggestions, oftentime unconsciously received, perhaps, which, like the deadly microbe that lays dormant in the human system until aroused to action by influences favorable to its ravages, became dominating influences in the mind of the negro, transforming him into a being full of suspicion, mistrust and, sometimes, hatred against the former trusted and respected master.

As before stated, the negro during his slave period was trustworthy and loyal to his master and his master's interests, and while it is claimed that he had great thieving proclivities, yet they usuallv pertained to something trivial; he would naturally say to himself: "Master's nigger and master's taters." Such privileges of taking something to eat could hardly be regarded in a strict sense as theft. This hereditary trait, born so innocently in slavery, might account for his great tendency to steal after slavery. For, how often the claim: "We worked and made it; it's as much ours as anybody's else!" A kind of community of interests feeling.

It is well known that the crime of rape was not heard of during slave-days, and many reasons have been offered to explain why this was, especially during and about the close of the Civil War when most of the white men were away, and the white women and children were left to the mercy of the negro. And even after he well knew that he would soon be set free, he still remained true to his trust, and was ready to defend, even at the cost of his life, the women and children left to his care.

It would not be amiss to say that the South should, as a fitting mark of gratitude and respect, erect a monument to the memory of the slave who was true and loyal to his invaluable trust.

THE EX-SLAVE NEGRO.

The influences must, indeed, have been strong that could transform the faithful and loyal slave of yesterday into the unfriendly, sullen and vindictive freedman of to-day. But such was the transformation. But while he hailed the announcement of liberation from bondage with outward demonstrations of joy, it is an undisputed fact that many of the race accepted the change of condition with some misgivings and fear, lest after all, the blessings of freedom might prove a curse in disguise. And it is well known that many did linger upon the old plantation, accepting such terms and upon such conditions as their former owners, in their impoverished state, could offer them; some of them never leaving, but being borne from their old cabin homes to the grave-yard on the hill hard by, where their ashes rest under the sod their feet in life had pressed.

Whether the negro, left free from extraneous influences, could have realized the truth so forcibly uttered recently by a negro orator from Yale, that "freedom is a process, and no man can be free until he has established for himself a character," is a question; but certain it is, that, without character or preparation this race was called upon to assume the role of a free man not only unprepared, but hedged about with every hindrance that could arise from innumerable adverse suggestions.

It is a well established scientific fact that those used to rendering obedience are the most susceptible to suggestion, both conscious and unconscious; hence, we have in the freedman a shining mark for a designing, mischief-making element, and how thoroughly and effectively the work was done, the conditions of to-day attest. And it may be as well understood now that we claim that to these agencies of discord, more than to all else, is due the deplorable position which this race occupies before the world to-day. Left to himself, the freedman was not a vicious person. There was nothing of malice in his nature toward the white race. But he was a creature easily duped, and his simple, untutored mind was a fertile soil for the reception of the seeds of wrong suggestion, and the ground was well sown. And how subtly were they sown! And how promptly did the tillers of this soil begin their work! Simultaneous with the home-coming of the remnants of Lee's and Johnson's armies was the arrival of these alien agitators. It is a matter of history, and, therefore, it is not necessary to quibble at this point, lest we display a sectional feeling, the South was absolutely overrun by designing politicians, over zealous and misguided philanthropists, and a horde of fortune hunters. And as we shall insist that, to the baleful suggestions received by the freedman, direct and indirect, intentionally given sometimes, and unintentionally at others, but always hurtful, is traceable, to a very large extent, the present unhappy state of the negro race, it is well to make our position plain.

The first suggestions the ex-slave received were of a material character. They were told that their labors had accumulated the wealth of the South prior to the war. What was left after the war was theirs, by right of conquest of the Union arms, and that the government would apportion it to them under a rule something like this: As one is to forty acres and a mule, so is the whole number to everything left. It was an adroit piece of calculation, and if the entire wealth of the country had been summed up at that time and apportioned according to the above calculation, the title to the bulk of the assets of the South would have been vested in the negro, however surprising this may have been to the inventor of the 40-acres-and-a-mule proposition. And this feeling of ownership was never eradicated; and if the negro has gained an unenviable reputation as a purloiner and a thief, it is but fair to say that, paradoxical as it may sound, he was and is, to a great extent, honestly so. It is well known that the Southern penitentiaries and chaingangs rapidly filled up just after the war between the States, and the inmates were largely negroes; and the records show that a large percentage of these were sent up for horse-stealing. Indeed, it became almost a mania among the race. Had the 40-acre-and-a-mule fallacy proven an indirect suggestion?

Along political lines was another avenue through which suggestion found easy access to the ex-slave's subjective mind. He was recognized as a full-fledged American citizen. He voted, held office, and was privileged to have a white man " 'rested " if he, the said white man, dared to molest him in the exercise of any of these political rights. And this state of being suggested to him the displacement of white rule entirely, and the usurpation of all authority of government—indeed, to the mind of the average negro, the South was soon to become the promised Canaan of the race, owned and dominated by the African contingent of American citizenship.

But the most baleful and fallacious of all direct suggestions that the ex-slave received about the time of his emancipation was that of social equality. We are not prepared to claim that, left to himself, the negro would never have entertained the thought, auto-suggestively. That faculty of imitation before referred to had enabled him to ape, in a crude way, as a rule, many of the manners and customs of the white folk. And many of his race had become men and women of intelligence; some had received more or less of an elementary education, and there were among them skilled workmen in all lines of mechanics. So that the recently liberated slave was far removed, in every respect, from his semi-savage forefathers.

Hence, what might have developed can only be surmised. But the correction of such suggestions, if they had arisen, would have been an easy matter, with the negro free from the false, devilish and, to his own better judgment, untenable suggestions.

The suggestion of social equality was received first from that same alien element who went among the freedmen immediately after the close of the Civil War, and, professing solicitude for their welfare, undertook to direct the recently liberated slaves in the setting in order of their social house. They discovered to the negro the fact that he was "Mister" So-and-so, not plain "Dick" or "Tom" of yesterday. They gave practical suggestive illustration then and there, by addressing him so, and sometimes the poor darkey was taken off his feet by being asked what his name was, that they might address him properly. He would blurt out some name hurriedly in his embarrassment, for he rarely ever assumed his late owner's name, to find later that, upon reflection, the name did not suit the cut of his jib and changed it, sometimes more than once. They further gave practical suggestion of equality by visiting the negroes in their cabins (generally under cover of darkness for obvious reasons), eating at table with them, and otherwise recognizing these relations. They were blarnied and cajoled by politicians and railroaded into office and given constant assurance of their superiority of caste.

All of these had a damaging effect, and while in thousands of instances the agitator failed to create a very high regard for himself in the estimation of the negro, yet, the feeling of disgust, often engendered, did not always afford counter suggestion sufficient to overcome the direct; for the reason, perhaps mainly, that the latter were in comport with the desires of the freedman.

Then there were other conditions that proved strong suggestions to the negro's mind, of the equality of the races socially. The mulatto was a living evidence of the maintenance of relations between the races in the past that should never exist between a superior and an inferior, between master and slave. And the sadness of the picture is intensified in the fact that the white man knew not how disastrously he was sowing the seeds of depravity, discord and disgrace. Sadly enough, they have had their reflex influence upon the white man. On account of these degrading and unhallowed relations the negro race came out of bondage, their women under clouds of unchastity, and both sexes alike holding the marriage relation in light esteem. This was the rule; of course, there were exceptions. Had the negro slaves been trained along lines of morality, chastity and right regard for these things, and had the whites maintained a proper moral relation to the blacks, the state of affairs above referred to would not have existed. To have encouraged the propagation of the species through promiscuous relations of the sexes was reprehensible, although justified on the ground of self-interest—every piccaninny represented so much assets of an estate.

And it is well known that healthy negro women were in demand for child-bearing.

And, while the ex-slave was slow in overt action upon these poisonous suggestions, they served to render him morose and sullen. He became restless, as if under a great restraint. He was suspicious of the white man, and incapacitated to enter into any business relations with his former master, with that feeling of confidence and desire for mutual good that is so essential to successful business intercourse. The suggestions he had received, both consciously and unconsciously, were to the effect that whatever of profit he proved to the white man thereafter, even in matters upon which his own subsistence depended, was undeserved; hence, there was, generally speaking, only a perfunctory rendering of service.

But time has righted many wrong suggestions in the case of the ex-slaves, at least. Unfortunately, their descendants have profited little by it. The years of constant association and business contact with Southern white men have brought about more amicable relations. Confidence has been restored in the mind of the ex-slave, and there exists a better understanding. And few of this class of negroes ever think of, or care for, closer social relations. And it is not this element that is responsible for the deplorable state of affairs existing; with the ex-slave only to deal with, the nation would have no "problem" for solution.

THE NEW NEGRO.

We have shown in preceding chapters some of the influences that surrounded the negro in slavery, and others that quickly followed emancipation; and, as we come to consider the "New Negro" of to-day, the question arises, has the progress of the race been commensurate with the opportunities? Has the advancement made during the first forty years of his freedom kept pace with his development during the slave period?

In order to arrive at a fair conclusion, let us see what progress had been made during the slave period. We have men of the race skilled in all lines of mechanics—every "quarter" had its carpenters, blacksmiths, tanners, harness and shoemakers, coopers, wagon-makers, etc.—and a majority of these had acquired more or less elementary learning. There were preachers, many of whom could read their texts and "line" the hymns, and, around every "big house" were butlers, coachmen, housekeepers, chambermaids and nurses who had, by close contact with their "white folks," learned much of the ways of the world outside of the slave domain. Few, comparatively, of the slave owners proscribed education among their slaves, and the children of these families were often the teachers from which their domestics and others often learned much that was of incalculable value in the years that followed. The youngsters or Miss of tender years seated at the nursery fireside, or in the play-yard shade, teaching a favorite servant, sometimes more than one, was a familiar picture in slavery days, and the heart of many an old ex-slave of to-day warms up, and there is seen a tender, far-away look of yearning, as if he would fain glance backward through the intervening years of the past half century or more, and once more contemplate the scene, long ago enacted, of young Marster or young Missus with diligence and patience unfolding to eager minds the mysteries of Webster's "blue back." How vividly is recalled the look of severity that for an instant beclouds the face of the young teacher, but is soon chased away by the sunshine of genuine interest—aye, affection—for the pupil who has failed to recite satisfactorily, or did not comprehend readily enough, the elucidation of some important lesson help! Perhaps it was that "K" might easily be recognized at any time, if the fact that its back was broken was kept in mind by the student.

Young master's body-servant was another favored slave, who profited much in many ways by his position. Sometimes he followed his master into professional life, and the opportunities for learning were exceptional. Indeed, it is safe to claim that hundreds of the race enjoyed these and like advantages. One thing we know: They were not all illiterate when they became freedmen. This is attested in the fact that all over the South, when martial law and bayonet rule essayed to fill many offices with negroes, there was an overflow of applicants for the "jobs" to let. Within a few months, Southern legislatures were overrun and dominated by negro politicians, courts were officered, and in all lines of public service the negro was in evidence.

From the semi-savage to the freedman, then, we find the negro well on the way to civilization, and somewhat enlightened, though he had been centuries learning the lesson.

Now the question recurs, what of the progress since emancipation?

In many respects the record is disappointing. In morals and in physical vigor the New Negro is far below the average of the ex-slave. And his intellect does not tower above that of his progenitors. True, he has enjoyed educational advantages—opportunities is, perhaps, a better word, for the greater body of the negro race is, comparatively, illiterate, and the census showing along this line is misleading. The "book-learning" of the freedman and his descendants is of a very shallow character, as applied to the masses.

There are a number of reasons for this. Short school terms in rural districts, the indisposition of the parents to take the children from the fields during the "cropping season," and too many colleges, are some of the potent reasons. The expenditure of vast sums in educational channels, upon comparatively few, whereas, if differently employed, the many would have received substantial profit, and all would have been benefited some, was a grave error. And the suggestion to the race thereby was unfortunate and damaging.

There have been established throughout the South too many colleges, universities and other institutions for the higher education of the negro. There is too much of display and glamor for the real article in learning. There are too many negroes who have been "thro' college," know much that is in books, and have imbibed a smattering of polish that are absolutely handicapped on account of the possession of a diploma. Why? The answer is simple: Auto-suggestion stands as a barrier between them and the only pursuits open to them. To these, "out in service" is not the thing. "It is too menial," says their auto-suggestion. And this applies, in large part, to those partially educated in the higher branches of learning, as well as to the graduate.

Writers and orators of the race, as well as others, lay great stress upon what education has done and is doing for the negro, but statistics, gathered and compiled from all the colleges, show that at the end of a generation of freedom only about 2,300 graduates have gone out from all the institutions of learning open to the race, including those graduated before the Civil War, and the tab kept upon the movements of these showed that little more than half of them were reported to be engaged in profitable pursuits.

Fifty-three per cent. of these were engaged in teaching, and sixteen per cent. were preachers. And this is the showing of a generation! This the returns of the millions that have been given with a free hand by benevolent and philanthropic people, individually and organic, for the sole purpose of education. Add to this the national schools and the school fund expended annually by every Southern State upon negro education, and the returns upon this fabulous expenditure are meagre indeed. The beginnings of the second generation found the race in about this condition: Two and seven-ninths per cent. graduates of colleges, and less than 50 per cent. with any education at all, while of this number a small percentage only were turning their education to account in their daily avocations. And many, as above shown, find their learning a drawback oftener than a help.

This, we admit, is an unfortunate state of affairs and to be deplored, but by it, the unwisdom of the plan of negro education adopted and pursued for forty years seems to be most clearly demonstrated. To attempt to charge the mind of the negro child, less than three centuries removed from the savage state, with schooling such as the white child is given, with twenty centuries of Christian civilization and enlightenment behind it, supplemented by constant intelligent individual effort, was, palpably, an impossibility, and a cruel exaction made upon a weakling intellect; and like many other conditions existing in our race relations, it is without a parallel in the history of nations.

Now, from these same institutions of learning have gone out some of the most hurtful and deplorable suggestions, as poisonous as they were fallacious, that have been imparted to the negro race through any medium, and by any agency. And they have been doubly damaging, in that they have begotten in a certain element of the white race counter suggestions, combative in their nature. When a negro boy or girl is taught to regard himself or herself as the social equal of white children, when his inner consciousness voices a counter suggestion, based upon his common sense, a state of feeling is engendered in the breast of that pupil that is to curse his or her life for all time, and that will work serious damage both to the individual and to the body politic of the race. Yet these suggestions, direct and indirect, are a part and parcel of the curriculum, if not laid down in the catalogue, well understood, of many such institutions; more prominent perhaps in some than in others. And, it seems that intelligent people—white teachers, many of them—even if no other motive than a desire for the welfare of the pupil prompted them, would modify that curriculum, at least. They are too intelligent to charge with ignorance in the matter. They are not blind to the results. It is one of the causes of the unfitness of the negro with an education, partial or finished, for the avocations open to his race. No self-respecting Southern white man will take a negro woman into his home, give her sleeping quarters upon the same floor with his family and conform to many other conditions precedent, as prescribed by some of these colleges which have an employment bureau attachment, and which furnish educated and trained domestics, because, forsooth, these conditions are designed as a moral safeguard for the servant. Northern sojourners in the South refuse to subscribe to such terms, and certainly Southern homes are not, as a rule, so constructed. Servants' quarters are so arranged as to prevent social contact. There must be no intercourse except as between employer and employee—a superior and an inferior. Other women of their race fill such positions without such "safeguards" and maintain their respectability, and are the equals of the college-bred domestics, barring education. But the educated or partially educated negro is but a slight percentage and not, by any means, the most dangerous element of the race. He has not heretofore figured much as a law-breaker, and, to be frank, he stands in more amicable relations to his white fellow-citizens than he has aforetime. There is more evidence of a desire on his part to co-operate in the efforts to suppress crime and bring criminals to account. And the time is short before the country will realize marked results from that co-operation. The example of a leading colored man, editor of a paper published in the interests of his race, prosecuting a colored woman before the courts in a Southern city for an alleged infraction of law, after repeated efforts to restrain her had been made, is an inspiring one. And he is on record as intending to keep it up. It is, he claims, in the interest of good morals among the race.

But it is more far-reaching than mere individual effort. Let the race—the vicious element, of course--learn that a few such men of their race in every community are on their tracks, and one of the most powerful counter suggestions to lawlessness and crime would take hold of the minds of the lawless and the restraining influences would be incalculably strong. Three determined and fearless leaders like this editor would do more toward putting a police recorder out of business than any city's "picked squad" of patrolmen.

So far, the influences of suggestion upon the colored race has been considered in a general way, without regard to any specific conditions or set of circumstances. There is a phase of the subject to which we now advert with the hope and belief that, though an oft threshed question, we shall be able to present some views upon a line hitherto disregarded, that may prove helpful in future discussions. It is that of

ASSAULT UPON WHITE WOMEN BY NEGRO MEN; ITS CAUSES AND PROPOSED RATIONAL REMEDIES.

The fact was mentiond, incidentally, in a former connection, that the crime of rape was seldom heard of during the slave period, and we will here add that this is accounted for most satisfactorily upon psychological grounds.

First, the "crime of rape," as used above, may be taken in a broader sense than the subject under discussion embraces. Let it apply to colored as well as white women, to facilitate the elucidation of the matter, and we shall see that there was an utter lack of suggestion in, or to, the negro man regarding the crime against either race of women, but upon entirely different hypotheses.

In the case of negro women there was absolutely no grounds for the basis of wrong suggestion, because none of the avenues of intercourse between the sexes were closed. While the marriage relations were entered into and maintained between negro men and negro women, these relations, on account of prevailing sentiment based upon customs, already referred to as wrong and degrading, were not essential to sexual intercourse. Hence, the conditions that might suggest rape were too remote to consider. The mind of the negro man was, therefore, free from improper suggestions as regards the women of his race. The other feature of the question, however, is as fraught with suggestion as this is devoid of it.

The first impression that found lodgment in the mind of the semi-savage when his foot pressed American soil was a conscious suggestion of inferiority.

(This is a conclusion fully justified upon several grounds. The fact that he was a slave, descended from the slave of black masters is sufficient to cite here.) And, above all else, the white Mistress of his new world was more an ideal object of worship than one to desecrate. And, as his sojourn lengthened into years, the queenly relations his white Mistress bore to the home, as well as to the whole social fabric, so far as his observation extended, fixed and strengthened this suggestion in his sub-conscious mind; so that the suggestion became a principle to be transmitted in a genealogical sequence, and, as the centuries passed, it became a bulwark of safety behind which was sheltered, unharmed, white women and children during the fateful sixties, when true and loyal black men all over the South not only worked faithfully for their subsistence, but bared their own brawny arms in defense of any of their "white folk" when danger was nigh.

Fortunate it is for the black man of the slave period that conditions were such as to preclude the idea or assumption that through fear a brutish nature was curbed and not because of his devotion to right and duty that the white Mistress passed through the slave period unassailed. During the Civil War the slaves at home, as a rule, were at all times fully apprised of the situation. There was (as a negro writer recently expressed it) a "free masonry" means of communication that kept them always informed.

Furthermore, in view of subsequent history, are we not justified in claiming that the war-time darkey—the ex-slave—has maintained a fair respectability since his emancipation? Some of their number have gone in forbidden ways, and penitentiaries have gathered many within their walls or on chaingangs, but the great body of the ex-slave element presents a fair record upon this question. In support of this claim, we cite the fact, which seems to have escaped observation, that the crime of rape does not belong to the slave period, neither is it a fruit of the ex-slave period proper. While there had been a few offenses of this character before, the crime was not so frequent as to arouse comment or create widespread alarm and consternation until many years after the emancipation of slavery. Therefore, it is fair and just to claim that the crime of assault is the crime of the "New Negro"—not of the slave nor of the ex-slave.

The grounds upon which we base the claim that "assault upon white women by negro men" is the crime of the "New Negro' we shall endeavor to make plain first; then we shall offer the proposed "Rational Remedies."

Suggestion, that subtlest of all agencies influencing, if not wholly dominating the human mind—dual in its nature—when rightly employed, is a great and moving power for good to the subject receiving it; and, through the subject, to everything with which it comes in touch, as illustrated in the career of the colored race, from the first importation of a slave to the emancipation of the race.

In striking, and sometimes alarming, contrast are the results of misdirected suggestion, or wrong suggestion of any form, whether direct of indirect; conscious or unconscious; intentional or unintentional. And to this influence of wrong suggestion we shall attempt to trace the source of the problem, at first sectional in its nature, but now involving the whole nation.

And it may be well to reiterate the claim before made, that to the alien element that overran the South immediately after the Civil War, and the influences that element set agoing in the minds of the negroes, more than to all else is traceable the trouble with the negro of to-day.

During the reconstruction period in the South, when the Federal authorities at Washington were engaged in amending the Constitution, passing civil rights bills, and otherwise working assiduously to bring about the fullest equality of races (some of these same leaders illustrating it in their private life) and their "officers of the line" were on the ground preaching this doctrine to the negroes, the very atmosphere in which the recently liberated slaves moved and which they breathed, was surcharged with the theme of race equality, and suggestions of future elevation ranging from "eating at the white folk's table" to amalgamation of the races, and even to a supremacy of the negro, were inhaled with every breath by the negro youth of the day, as well as the elders of his people. While the fathers among them were less susceptible to the infection, by virtue of a lifetime of positive direct counter suggestion, minds of the youth of the day were free and open to take in and assimilate the poison of the suggestions so assiduously sown by alien political emissaries of the powers at Washington, and so faithfully taught in the schools by white men and women from the North, who, also, maintained these social relations toward the negro in their private lives, so far as the laws of the land would permit and publicly, so far as Southern sentiment would tolerate.

Subsidiary to the work of the agitator, was the mother's influence in implanting these seeds of social equality suggestions in the minds of her children. But a great degree of tolerance should be employed in considering this phase of the subject. The mother-heart of the slave woman must have thrilled with unwonted emotions of joy at the thought that the dawn of liberty had opened upon her race while her offspring were just entering upon life, and even if she had passed by youth and middle life in slavery, she had the happy consciousness that, in her declining years, the home of a freeman would be to her a shelter, and out of it she would be borne to her grave. This, she knew, was a reality; and with the reality had come the promise of higher ascension in the scale of social life for her children; they were "good as any white children"—better than "po' white trash." That she should strengthen these suggestions by every means possible, in the minds of her children, was natural, and she did more, the infant of the day drew the inspiration from the mother's breast with every drop of its milk food. And, while there were doubts and misgivings in the mind of the intelligent colored man, he hesitated to discountenance these suggestions. His intelligence suggested strongly to his mind that the only logical outcome of the policy of reconstructionists at Washington was social equality, miscegenation and amalgamation. Of course, this carried with it a terrible conviction; it meant bloodshed as well; but were not the Federal armies behind the movement? thought he.

Amid these surroundings the young negro began life. Schools all over the South were established and with their establishment every influence that could be conceived was brought to play upon the mind of negro children to create the impression that they, as beneficiaries of the school privileges, were indebted solely to their Northern white friends for them; that the Southern whites were not only antagonistic to negro education, but were hostile to everything that tended to the betterment of the race. And, in many instances, the jealousy of the white people of the negro's advancement was charged on the ground that they feared the negro's development would result finally in the superiority of the negro race; thus, the suggestion of negro supremacy obtained a strong position in the minds of many negroes. How familiar became the claim that "the bottom rail" would soon be "on top."

In all of these things the negro felt that the people at the North were in full sympathy and accord with all that was being done. That the policy pursued by the Johnson administration, for the establishment of a social scale in the South that recognized and tolerated no distinction on account of race, color, etc., met the unqualified approval of every Northern citizen. But, if such was the case, then (and we are not disposed to believe it) there came in due time a revulsion of feeling. There came a time when the mismanagement of the misguided extremists at the North, and the false and (sometimes) incendiary suggestions of their emissaries at the South, became apparent. It was when the habitation of the black race was no longer circumscribed to the country south of the Ohio river. When he had gained a footing more or less well established in almost all of the States in the Union. Then it was that the people of the whole country began to understand the situation, and sentiment became changed.

Growing up in this atmosphere of training the New Negro was wholly unprepared to meet the actual realities that the future developed. Social elevation did not come to him, along with the education he had received. His black skin was, as much as ever, the mark of inferiority of race. Years passed, he became a man physically. Instead of an open field in the social realm, he was as much circumscribed as ever; the white man had maintained that superiority which, by every right vested in a superior race, he claimed was his. Public sentiment at the same time at the North was overwhelmingly with the Southern white men (although it was some years later before it became active), and the negro realized in the situation as it was that the foolish fallacies implanted in his young mind were but bubbles that burst before the blasts of reason in later years. And, with this revelation, came a most dangerous suggestion. It was, that the negro was being robbed of a right that, according to suggestions in a thousand ways imparted, he had come to regard as his; that, on account of the duplicity of the white race, he still occupied an inferior position, and never once admitting to himself that former suggestions were perhaps erroneous. And, brooding over these imaginary wrongs (being unable rather than unwilling to apply the light of reason), the deadly and damning suggestion of the employment of force to accomplish a right of which sentiment robs him and not law forbids him, was implanted in his mind. We say "his mind" advisedly, for the outcropping does not by any means discover to view the extent of the existence of these dark suggestions. They are manifested upon the streets, along the highways, around the homes—everywhere—throughout the South, daily, and in an unmistakable manner. These manifestations are not unnoticed by the whites, and doubtless many a tragedy is averted, and many a dark crime is forestalled because they are noted. Lack of opportunity often, and lack of brute courage sometimes, and an increasing watchfulness all the time, has preserved the honor of far more white women of the country than have suffered the loss of it at the hands of the rapist.

SUGGESTION AS A SOLUTION.

We come now to consider a solution for this most absorbing problem with a degree of satisfaction on account of the fact that the change of sentiment regarding the race question, which has been very marked, even radical, during the past few years in certain sections, will contribute much towards that solution. During recent years the people of the other sections of the Union have had a meed of the experience in dealing with the rapist negro, that the South has so long contended with. The country at large has come to a knowledge of the situation in a sense most calculated to carry conviction. The sojourn of the negroes at the North (and by this term is meant all sections before unused to the negro as he is known at the South), has proven a revelation to the masses. Seeing him as he is has been a convincing proof of his unfitness for social equality. The horror at the thought of miscegenation and amalgamation experienced only at the South at first, is shared now throughout the country. The expediency of it is not only denied at the North, but the proposition is revolting alike to the respectable white element everywhere.

The formula of the remedy for the malady once agreed upon, its faithful application and patience will bring the desired results. For, it may be well borne in mind, that the disease not being at an acute stage, but of a chronic type, it can not be overcome in a day, but will require time for its eradication.

First, as an all-important basis: If, as we have shown, suggestion has played so important a part in shaping the destiny of the negro race, figuring in every phase of his career, from the semi-savage state until this day, then, through the same medium, much toward the solution of the problem may be accomplished.

While the problem has become a national one, in a strict sense, it must be admitted that upon the South mainly, devolves the responsibility of a solution. This may appear paradoxical, taken in connection with the claim, heretofore made, that to northern sentiment and northern interference with local affairs was chargeable the present status of the race. But in our support of that claim, the distinction between the two was made clear, and the change of sentiment at the North has not only removed all support of the claim to social equality for the negro, but has gone a long way toward creating a strong counter suggestion in the mind of the New Negro upon that subject. In fact, there is less of a desire upon the part of the respectable element of the race for social equality than ever before. The conviction, once so thoroughly entrenched in the mind of the negro, that such relations should not exist, and never eradicated, but rather overshadowed, for the time being, is rapidly reasserting itself and claiming recognition—how? Auto-suggestively.

One of the first steps employed in furtherance of the radical plans adopted for the reconstruction of the Southern States, was the wholesale enfranchisement of the negro, without regard to his fitness for the exercise of suffrage. Subsequent history has demonstrated that this was a grievous error, and his right of suffrage should have been admitted only after he had demonstrated such qualifications, moral and mental, as would enable him to exercise it intelligently. This would have been fair to all classes of the race. The negro who possessed such qualifications at the outset would have been enfranchised, while the ignorant and incompetent element so largely in the majority, would have been barred until such time as he was enabled to subscribe to the conditions of qualification. Had this been done, the suggestions of right deportment, and high moral and mental attainment, in other words, the suggestion of good citizenship would have been paramount in the mind of the negro, instead of the seriously erroneous suggestions he did receive in this connection, to which we have referred. But the proposition to repeal the voting clause of the Constitution of the United States relative to the negro, at this late day, is as manifestly wrong as the act was erroneous at first.

First, it would work a hardship upon a strong element of the race who, by thrift and enterprise, have property rights at stake, and until more of the race not so fortunate, perhaps, but whose intelligence and learning, as well as their moral status, entitle them to recognition as good citizens; and, second, because every State in the Union enjoys the rights necessary to regulate suffrage by legislation, and all of them affected do enact such laws as are necessary to regulate the franchise of its citizens, "without regard to race, color," etc., it is true, but quite effective in eliminating the incompetent voters, both white and colored, Disfranchisement, therefore, is not expedient.

It is unfortunate that intelligent negro writers and speakers keep up such a fusilade of attack upon white people for alleged suppression of the negro ballot, when their common sense teaches them that such is not the case. There is no effort on the part of the whites to suppress a single legal vote of the race in any regular election. Democratic primary, or nominating elections in practice in the South, are not "regular" legal elections, and if the negro is excluded in these, so is his white brother of the Republican party. And these always have the right to bring out a Republican ticket and contest in the election proper, the election of the ticket endorsed by the opposition.

These are political party questions and not race questions. The negro is simply afflicted with the weaker party in politics. And this, from a choice made years ago, and it is unfair to the weaker element of his race that these practices are resorted to by his intellectually stronger brother; for they are taken seriously by these auditors, and if the applause they receive is gratifying, they should understand it is at great cost to the cause they represent. Suggestion of a damaging character is begotten—half suppressed truth, becomes blatant falsehood. Open, fair dealing with all questions by negro leaders is demanded by every sense of right.

The negro's status before the law is wrongly dealt with by this same element. Every intelligent being shows that the courts of the country, from the desk-room notary publics, to the Supreme Court of the United States, are open to him, and legal counsel is his, upon demand, before any one of these tribunals. The preaching of negro oppression by the courts should be restrained, if necessary, by the broadening of jurisdiction in contempt proceedings, so as to take in the agitator, and thus suppress a very strong and hurtful suggestion.

A recent enactment of a very stringent vagrancy law by the Georgia Legislature was vigorously attacked by a leading Atlanta negro preacher, on the ground that it was "aimed at" the colored race; when he well knew that not a syllable of the act applied to the negro that did not mean as much to the white race. That, if it affected the negro more seriously than it did the whites, it was because there were more negro vagrants than white vagrants. Therefore, the course of the preacher was attacked in the columns of a newspaper and his utterances were given wide publicity among the negroes. The more strongly to be condemed are these utterances, because they were so widely at variance with the spirit of the occasion, which was a gathering of leading white and colored men engaged in the discussion of ways and means for the elevation and betterment of his race; a notable and leading spirit present being his own church bishop. The closing of dance-halls, where vice and immorality prevailed among his race, was as strongly protested against on this same occasion by the preacher, because, he claimed, it was the oppression of the negro, and it abridged his rights. This in the face of the fact that reputable people of his own race joined in invoking the law's action on the grounds of it being a nuisance and a menace to the peace and good order of the city.

While it is not probable that there were present many of the class that could be seriously affected by the preacher's inopportune and foolish remarks, it is true that a newspaper comment was a vehicle that carried them broadcast, and the damage done was serious and far-reaching, counteracting much of the real good accomplished at the series of meetings, of which this was one.

What a revolution of sentiment the cessation of these and like practices would work! What a strong current of counter-suggestion would be set in motion if these same gifted writers and eloquent speakers turned their efforts into more rational and conservative channels!

In the South, at least, the rapist in almost all instances of outbreak, comes from the ranks of the vagrant—the lowest element of the negro race. The rural districts are his field of operations, and he wanders through the country, ostensibly in search of employment, but in reality bent only upon mischief. He does not hesitate at theft, burglary, arson, or criminal outrage—whatever seems to promise success, even murder, if necessary to accomplish any of these designs, or to cover up a crime. This is the rule; occasionally he is one well known in the community, and often he is one of the migratory class, whose stay on some man's plantation has been of a sufficient duration to localize him enough to be regarded as a member of the community, but which stay was only long enough to enable him to accomplish some deep and devilish purpose.

The remedy for this class is: First, clean towns and cities where such low resorts as afford them shelter, can not exist; strict laws against idleness, and a nomadic life, and fearless execution of those laws. Second, the respectable working colored man and woman should discountenance these people in their worthless manner of living. Let these understand that they can no longer expect shield or support from this better class, and the effect would be marvelous. It is inexplicable, but true, that it is the disposition of negroes generally, to aid the criminal of the race to escape, rather than to hand him over to justice. It is a well-known fact that it is almost impossible for a white man to go into any quarter of a city where negroes live, and ascertain the whereabouts of a negro, though he may inquire of those living in the immediate vicinity, even of next-door neighbors. Negroes will shield the worst criminal of their race from detection and arrest, though a stranger, while the white man will hand his next-door neighbor over to justice when implicated in crime.

We have in the foregoing an illustration of a suggestion implanted during the slave period, and doubtless at an early date. But the negroes should put away those old slave-time customs of shielding the "run-away nigger." How tenacious the hold of a suggestion when once rooted in the human mind!

The law to put down and drive out the loafer, and suppress his rendezvous, and the respectable negroes upholding that law, by every suggestion to the vagrant, that he may no longer look for or expect recognition and aid in his manner of living, are the country's strongest levers for uprooting this incubus on society.

Then there is that other element of the rapist negro, less numerous, but dangerous, because, under the guise of respectability, the negro servant who, by virtue of his domestic employment, is constantly in contact with the women of the home. Unfortunately, these are often less careful of his presence than they should be. The old slavery-day customs of careless indifference to the presence of the morning fire-builder in female apartments, and like opportunities for observation of the persons of the white Mistress and the young Misses of the home, may have been responsible in a far greater measure for the latter day crime than it would be pleasant to admit. The suggestion of safety then implanted in the white Mistress' mind has been handed down even to the present day, and it is a fact that there is too much indifference yet existing along this line, in the face of the dangers that menace the safety of white women. It is unfortunate, and the source of much harm, that the Southern Mistress failed to recognize that the freedman was not her slave, but her former slave, and to treat him as such. But instead, old customs prevailed, and while the freedman maintained his integrity as a rule (many did not), the new negro received and cherished strong suggestions from this source.

Remove the contact, often too close, in the home; in business relations; in close-seated vehicles "built for two"; on the farm, where too often girls and young women "hoe their rows," or pick cotton alongside the negro man—sometimes wholly at his mercy, (and often becoming his victim)—and separate the races in factories and workshops; let the negro janitor go from schools and colleges where girls are in attendance, and female teachers are employed; in a word, let Southern people recognize in the "New Negro" a person far removed from the darkey of other days, and a suggestion that breeds deadliest poison in the mind of this new creature will be removed.

It is this class of negroes most subject to the suggestion begotten by disapppointment in the development of race conditions, that the race has been robbed of rights by unfair methods, and he is impelled by a desire to possess and drag down the object of his lust to his own low level, not only by lutsful desires, but by a spirit of revengeful hatred.

Race separation upon any conceivable plan, although strongly advocated by a few, among whom is a leading negro bishop of the African Methodist Episcopal Church, and a Southern newspaper editor of note as a platform speaker, seems too chimerical to consider as a remedy in this connection. The negro does not wish to leave the country—not many of his race—and there are no legal avenues open to deportation; and unless he could be legally deported, or could be induced to voluntarily clear our shores, in a body, the proposition fails of materialization.

From the first proposition there is little to expect. And as regards the latter, an incident illustrative of the negro's resourcefulness in expediencies, aptly sets forth his position in the premises: An old negro who was serving a term in prison for the offense of horse-stealing, was constantly upbraiding his fellow-prisoners for their deeds, which had brought them into prison. He was particularly abusive of a certain one who happened to be serving a term for perhaps the same offense as his own. After submitting to a round of abuse, one day, more severe than usual, the fellow-prisoner stopped the old man and said: "Now, look here, I admit you are right; my crime was a bad one, but what did you come here for?" This was sudden and unexpected, but the old fellow was equal to the demands upon him, and he replied: "Didn't come here; white folks fotch me here."

With the negro here to stay, whatever is accomplished in the way of a solution of this vexed problem must, to prove successful, have his co-operation. In the pulpit, in the public prints, in politics and at home, a demand is upon him to bend his intelligent efforts in the direction of bringing the weaker element of his race up to his own level of moral and intellectual standing. The hurtful and vicious suggestions that have so strongly figured in the past, must be met and overcome by counter-suggestions.

The intensely religious nature of the negro is an excellent avenue through which to inculcate the religious principle that demands good citizenship. The Divine command: "Let every soul be subject unto the Higher Powers," carries with it no qualification. We should not "despise those in authority." To cease from abuse of governmental institutions and men in authority would convey strong suggestion. In a word, counter-suggestion that will stop decline, arrest and restrain the vicious before actual outbreak, is the hope.

Neither social nor political relations of a close nature are desirable to the intellectual colored man. The stamp that differentiates the races is as apparent to the negro as to the white man. There is a relation, however, that is most desirable to both the fair-minded negro and the honest white man. It is a cordial, neighborly relation, that admits of free, open business intercourse, without any apprehension on the part of either of unfair methods being employed. Upon the white man more than upon the black, rests the responsibility. He is in position to invite this, by indirect suggestion, which must, and surely will, flow out of earnest effort upon his part. Let the negro understand that he will receive honest compensation for services rendered, and how readily he will respond! He is so constituted; his confidence once won, his faithfulness is as strong as his emotional nature can make it. Let the negro understand that the white man is not jealous of his attainments. The fact that he does favor education among the race is strongly suggested by his willingness to pay taxes for that purpose.

There is an element that has received no notice during this discussion, because his influence is of no effect, pro or con, upon the race problem; it is the low white class. His vacillating and unstable character robs him of any influence among the intelligent, upright citizens of either race, and the law that restrains and punishes the vicious blacks, operates with equal force in his case.

The intelligent and upright people of the two races must meet this question, each in his particular sphere, and honest effort and patient waiting upon right suggestion will bring about a happy solution.

THE NEGRO NOT A BEAST.

A solution of the negro problem psychologically considered has, without any special effort, proved that the negro is not "a beast," notwithstanding an effort has been made to prove otherwise by distorting the Bible with disconnected sentences and phrases which are used for Biblical proof. The whole religious world may hide its face in shame and disgust at the thought that any one should be so sacrilegious as to try to use the Bible for such an unhallowed purpose.

As we have pointed out in the first part of this psychological treatise, "every human being is endowed with a dual mind, namely, objective and subjective. The objective, or reasoning mind, is controlled by the five senses (seeing, hearing, feeling, etc.), and is the outgrowth of man's physical necessities. It is his guide in his struggles with material environments. The objective mind has for its highest function, reasoning. The subjective mind takes cognizance of its environment by means independent of the five physical senses. It perceives by intuition. It is the seat of emotions; it is the storehouse of memory. This duality of the mind renders man susceptible to all kinds of suggestions known to the realm of psychology."

If we wish to draw an analogy from the Bible, it would be more in keeping with the eternal fitness of things to show that the internal evidences of the Bible are a greater and more conclusive argument of its own authenticity than the evidences deduced by natural theology ,or by prophecy, or by reasoning, so with the negro it did not seem necessary to prove that he was a man, or of the genus homo, because this is not only an admitted fact, but it is a self-evident fact.

In the chapter on his semi-savage state, where he is viewed in his lowest mental development, it is clearly shown that he is highly susceptible to suggestion, under the same psychological laws as all other human beings, and by the immutable laws of suggestion, he has made progress along the lines of mental development. His objective mind has increased in proportion that his physical necessities have dictated. His subjective mind seems to predominate in his semi-savage state, owing to the fact that his reasoning faculties were weak for want of cultivation and a chance to develop. Hence, the proverbial intuition of the old darkey, which is often imitated by writers, and quoted as "Uncle Dick's Philosophy."

Since the negro has had an opportunity to cultivate his objective or reasoning mind, like all other human beings, he does not depend so much on his intuition or subjective mind, but is able to employ his reasoning faculties according to the same laws that govern his Caucasian friend. It is under this law that the negro is capable, if not hindered by wrong suggestion, to attain to still higher development, mentally, morally and religiously. If too much is expected of him, the responsibilities will have a tendency to dethrone his reason from the fact that he is only in the primary or undeveloped mental stage.

It is hoped that all good people, both white and black, will realize that a great problem confronts them, and in proportion with the right suggestion, as given to the weaker race, only a few years removed from savagery, in that proportion will the problem be solved.